MINE TO DIE

MINE
TO
DIE

Rob Donovan

Troubador Publishing Ltd
Unit E2 Airfield Business Park,
Harrison Road, Market Harborough,
Leicestershire. LE16 7UL
Tel: 0116 2792299
Email: books@troubador.co.uk
Web: www.troubador.co.uk/matador

ISBN 978 1805142 829

British Library Cataloguing in Publication Data.
A catalogue record for this book is available from the British Library.

Printed and bound in the UK by TJ Books Limited, Padstow, Cornwall
Typeset in 11pt Minion Pro by Troubador Publishing Ltd, Leicester, UK

THIS WORK – *MINE TO DIE* –
IS DEDICATED TO MY FRIEND

JOHN TOMAN

**Former Chief Mining Surveyor at South Crofty Mine,
Relief Mine Captain and a Man of God**

SECTIONS OF THE BOOK

OVERTURE

Feelings of trepidation and excitement – that's a good blend for starting a book. I do know, after all, where I am going. Underground. Under the surface of things. And I am starting with an overture.

An overture is something offered to open the way to some conclusion. The word 'overture' comes to us from the Old French *overture*, meaning 'opening, proposal'. This Old French word is rooted in the Latin *apertura*, meaning 'opening', from *aperire*, 'to open, uncover'. There we have it. Open, and under we go. My task is to create a book that will be called *Mine to Die* and in it I shall offer an account of the industrial revolution that transformed the landscape in one county of England, Cornwall, through mining the ground under its surface.

You will find that each section of my book also begins with an overture, a page or more of source material for you to read and make your own interconnections before taking on board the commentary that follows.

All will become clear. Trust me, if you dare – I am a maker of magic; a wordsmith intent on offering the reader my take on our history over the last 250 years. A magician who is a qualified historian. I know my trade. I weave my tales of understanding through the selection of data I call facts – and so they are, no matter how random their pathway to my being. I want to recreate the past in such a way that my tale is faithful to the historical record and, at the same time, enables you to be present in that past.

Nevertheless, you are your own historian. You can choose to create your own tapestry of interpretations. But please keep an open mind. Humility is a virtue for those who follow the trade of history making.

When I became a teenager around sixty years ago, I acquired a book that claimed to tell the history of England. I still have the volume. In it, industrialisation is presented as an agency for welfare, serving to nourish and clothe the people. That is very far from being the whole truth, as the analysis in my book will show. Industrialisation brought sickness, injury, and death, too.

I want to weave a tale in these pages that will draw you into what I consider a most absorbing and important question. I promise you a novel kind of history making and telling, but I will be frank. In the end, I am hoping you will make a judgement call that is in favour of life and against the unregulated pursuit of profit when faced with this ethical question: Should the pursuit of profit ever be at the expense of health, well-being, and life itself?

These concerns could not be more vital. The industrial revolution that began a quarter of a millennium ago in Britain now threatens to extinguish our global existence as a species.

Let me introduce you now to one of my important sources for this venture into history: nineteenth and twentieth-century broadsheet newspapers. They had the space for the editors to publish much of the copy produced by reporters at public meetings. These reporters were good at recording the words of participants. Such a factual record has been illuminating. The story I weave through time – from the second half of the nineteenth century through to the killing fields of the First World War and then through the end-time of tin mining in the rest of the twentieth century – will have a local Cornish focus, but it also serves as a study in microcosm of what has been happening in capitalist industrial societies over the last 250 years: the pursuit of profit by the few at the expense of the health and well-being of the masses. Such wording risks being too simplistic; the analysis needs more subtlety – but at times it comes down to that sort of ruthless focus.

My book is divided into sections, many of which begin with newspaper stories taken from the resources of The British Newspaper Archive (BNA). This is free to search in the British Library reading rooms but has also been made available to read online at home. The teams of people who have been employed to digitise individual newspaper pages come at a cost and I have paid my subscription to gain full access. I did so when I was alerted in the autumn of 2021 to the news that copies of *The Cornish Post and Mining News*, published from 1889 to 1944 in Camborne, the centre of the Cornish mining industry, had been digitised and were now available.

At that moment, the idea for this book began to germinate. And I soon discovered my searches were yielding rich data from other publications too. This idea of mine was bearing fruit. I knew now that this would be a book worth reading.

Here is the first of my sections, with a selection of its sources presented and acknowledged, followed by my commentary. The overture has concluded; the journey begins.

THESE PEOPLE ARE NOT LIKE US

Source: *Camborne / The Cornish Telegraph /* Thursday 21 November 1889

Sent to Prison

Messrs. W. Pike and W. Rabling, presiding magistrates, on Wednesday committed Joseph Henry Thomas of Camborne, to prison for fourteen days for being drunk and disorderly on Tuesday night, and another fourteen days for assaulting the police.

Sudden Death of a Miner

While James Mager, of Tuckingmill, was working on the dressing floors of Carn Brea Mine on Friday blood suddenly poured from his mouth, and he fell to the ground and died in a quarter hour. Deceased, who in consequence of ulceration of the lungs had to give up underground work, was 27 years old, and leaves a wife and child.

Concert

A concert was given at Pengegon Wesleyan Chapel, on Thursday evening by the chapel choir, assisted by members of the Philharmonic band, numbering in all about forty. The solo parts were taken by Miss Bennetts, soprano; Miss Vivian, contralto, Mr. Prosser, tenor; and Messrs. Warren and Pearce, bass. There was a large attendance, and Mr. F. Miller conducted.

Some scene-setting for starters. There was a time when there were neither engine or boiler houses, nor mine shaft rigs or arsenic-burning chimneys in the south-west Cornish landscape. Until the late seventeenth century, most of the area had been covered by thick woodland. Then came the axeman. The need for timber generated by the expanding mining industry, not least as props to stop the mine shafts and tunnels from collapsing, created a new landscape.

There were, however, areas of woodland that did survive. They remained, for instance, in the estates of those Cornish landed aristocracy and gentry who used their acres of trees as both game reserve and a barrier. These swathes of woodland served as a boundary between themselves and the mining, farming, and fishing communities, who lived out their hard and often shorter lives on the other side. "These people are not like us" are words that either side could have said about the other, either in tones of superiority or in a spirit of deference.

Nevertheless, this physical separation between the two worlds masked important connections between the wealthy elite and those beneath them in a social hierarchy that had been ordained by those who had held power over generations.

Tehidy Park and House, Illogan, near Camborne – early nineteenth century engraving. This is the neo-classical Georgian house created by Francis Basset (1757-1835). It was rebuilt between 1861 and 1863 by John Francis Basset (1831-1869)[1]

Land ownership was the critical factor. Take the case of the Bassets, who had obtained the manor of Tehidy around the middle of the twelfth century. They lived in their Tehidy manor house until a larger mansion was begun in 1734, built largely on the profits from the copper and tin that was mined from under the ground of their manor. Such metallic ores were theirs to exploit.

The Camborne local historian, Michael Tangye, tells a remarkable story in *Tehidy and the Bassets – The Rise and Fall of a Great Cornish Family* (1984/2002). Francis Basset succeeded to the lordship of the manor in 1769, took the title of Lord de Dunstanville, and set out to remodel the mansion

---

1   Source: Courtesy of the DiCamillo Companion

*Dolcoath Copper mine, Camborne – an 1831 engraving, showing the 1776
engine house with capstan alongside, together with launder and bal.[2]*

as the finest house in Cornwall and create a way of living
that mirrored the most expensive and elegant of any elite
Georgian family in London, or elsewhere in the country. He
could, after all, consider himself to be the richest man in the
county. Just under ninety years later, in 1855, John Francis
Basset succeeded to these Tehidy estates and before his death
in 1869, he was responsible for another rebuild of what now
became a great Victorian country house. The money to
finance this expenditure came from the Basset mines and
from land rents. Since most of the copper had been mined,
it was the tin that lay underneath the copper which now
underpinned the Basset wealth. Of all their mines, it was
the Dolcoath Mine in Camborne that proved their biggest
money-spinner in this new world of tin extraction.

You will find I have given the Victorian Bassets a section

2   Source: Wikipedia

of their own in my history book. They are of seminal importance in considering my question of the relative value of human life and health on the one hand and the accumulation of wealth on the other. Suffice to say at this point that the so-called great family of the Bassets were beset by mental health issues that were assumed to be genetic. Arthur, the brother of John Francis Basset, inherited the estates in February 1869; thirteen months later, Arthur had committed suicide in a London asylum. The next brother in line, Gustavus, then became the lord of the manor and before his death in 1888 from throat and lip cancer, made certain in 1880 that the fourth and youngest brother, Walter, was declared of unsound mind. With Walter ruled insane, Gustavus's son, Arthur Francis, who had been born in 1873, became the first direct heir to succeed for a century or more. There were stories within the estate that Mrs Basset had gone on holiday to their estate in Scotland and returned with a baby boy – Arthur Francis – who everyone thought must have been adopted. Be that as it may, he was brought up in the manner fitting a Basset.

Less than thirty years later, in November 1916, as world war raged and scores of young men from Camborne died in the trenches across the Channel, Arthur Francis Basset, now deep in debt from gambling on horse racing and already a largely absentee lord of the manor, sold the mansion and all the rest of the estate with its houses, farms, and mines. Three years later, an unexplained fire left the mansion a ruin.

The Basset story serves as an exiguous example of how power and wealth could be lost in a world where so much was changing. Arthur Francis Basset had been brought low by self-indulgence and an addiction to gambling, but the fate of his business affairs was determined by the decline in the price of tin in the late Victorian and early Edwardian period, and then by the exigencies of war. His mining staff had expertise, but they could not control what was happening elsewhere in the world, in Asia and the Americas and then Europe. In such circumstances, it was no surprise that at least some of those who had been the beneficiaries of the unregulated Victorian pursuit of profit came a cropper.

Tehidy House after the great fire of 26th February 1919. The fire is still smouldering and firefighters with the Redruth fire engine can be seen tackling the blaze, watched by onlookers.[3]

The town of Camborne is situated less than three miles south of Tehidy and around three miles from the coast of the Atlantic, on the side of a hill sloping towards the north-west,

3 Source: www.imagearchive.royalcornwallmuseum.org.uk

between 300 and 400 feet above the level of the sea. A report in the *Royal Cornwall Gazette* of a public meeting on Friday, 12 August 1864, quoting from a petition to adopt the Local Government Act of that year, stated that at the last census (in 1861) the parish of Camborne contained a population of 14,040, '*principally miners who are an industrious, provident, and cleanly class of persons.*' The town of Camborne, together with the neighbouring village of Tuckingmill, lay in the centre of this parish and had a population of 7,474, an average-sized Victorian industrial town at the time, although such a calculation needs to consider that as many miners were living outside the confines of the town, in neighbouring villages, as within it. The petitioners were at pains to point out that within the town:

'*...places are well laid out, the streets being wide and the houses commodious, and by no means crowded together; nor is there an excess of population for the number of dwellings, there being 1,791 houses to contain the 7,474 inhabitants.*'

Such a description would make good copy in the tourist industry that lay around the historical corner: 'Come to healthy Cornwall. See the industrial sights. Admire our local miners, a class of persons, a form of life, whose cleanliness brings them ever closer to God Almighty.'

But the petitioners knew that there was muck behind the mask. Deaths in Camborne between 1860 and 1863 were thirty-three per cent more than expected. "This fearful mortality is quite unnecessary," these good men of the urban elite proclaimed – and went on to lay the blame on "the want of a sufficient supply of water, and of an efficient system of drainage." The remedy, they said, was for Camborne to adopt the Local Government Act. This Act was the Improvement of Land Act of 1864.

A Public Works Act, which provided for relief of poverty through schemes of local works such as road maintenance, had been passed in 1863, the year before. That Act of Parliament had been a consequence of the American Civil War (1861-65), which had led to the Lancashire Cotton Famine. The Lancashire cotton industry had experienced a massive decline in imports of raw cotton from the USA due to the war, leading to a severe economic and social crisis that was particularly acute between 1861 and 1864. The distress of the cotton workers, who were now unemployed or on short time, placed unbearable strains on the poor-law guardians, who were responsible for putting a roof over the head of those now made homeless, and the relief committees who were responsible for distributing private charity. It was time for the national government to intervene to ameliorate the adverse effects of a global market economy.

It was in this climate of reform, born of necessity, that the Improvement of Land Act of 1864 had legislated for the building and improvement of local sewers, drains, watercourses, and the like. But any new powers that arose from these Acts were permissive, not compulsory. They provided a template but the decision to put the recommendations into practice remained with the local authority. This emphasis on the permissive rather than the mandatory remained the case over a decade later when the Tory prime minister, Benjamin Disraeli, ensured the passing of the Public Health Act of 1875. This legislation did help limit the spread of many diseases, such as cholera and typhoid, but it was still left to the local authorities to make the decision to act. Hence, the public meeting in August 1864 in Camborne to discuss the petition to adopt the legislation of that year – and the raucous nature of that gathering.

The petitioners were convinced that this Act should be implemented. People's lives could be saved. But for others, the cost was too high. Captain Charles Thomas Junior (1832-1896), of Tuckingmill, earnestly opposed its adoption. He called himself Captain Charles Thomas Junior to distinguish himself from Captain Charles Thomas Senior (1795-1868). They called themselves Captain by dint of their roles as mines' agents; they were the managers, stewards for the mine owners and other adventurers who had invested capital in the enterprise. Charles Thomas Senior was not the father of Charles Thomas Junior; Josiah Thomas (1833-1901) was the son of Charles Thomas Senior and we will encounter Josiah later in this book, as we will Frederick W. Thomas (1863-1931), the son of Josiah Thomas and grandson of Charles Thomas Senior. All these men bearing the name Thomas had connections with the Bassets and Dolcoath.

Charles Thomas Senior was the mine agent at Dolcoath, who had achieved fame and reward by convincing the Basset owners and other investors to sink the mine deeper to reach the tin lodes he was convinced were present, now the copper was becoming exhausted. In 1836, Captain Charles Thomas had drawn up the first of his plans, but it took nearly two decades to persuade those who had the finances to commit to the deeper mine. Not until 1853 was the first dividend

paid on the tin that was now being extracted. My source –
The Great Dolcoath by Albert Bluett (1898, Camborne Old
Cornwall Society) – provides the detail that:

> '...the value of the mine, calculated on the market
> price of shares, rose from £4,000 in 1846, to £90,000
> in 1868, and during the intervening period £147,854
> was paid in dividends to the shareholders.'[4]

The Bassets, and those who helped finance them, were sitting
on a proverbial gold mine, in the form of tin.

Captain Charles Thomas Junior was, in his own right,
also an important and powerful local figure. As a manager at
the Dolcoath mine, his job was to keep a close eye on all the
miners under his control and ensure they and their families
extracted and processed the metallic ores in a fitting manner.
In 1864, Captain Thomas was thirty-two years old and lived
in Pendarves Street, in an upmarket part of Camborne, with
his wife and growing family. The 1861 national census tells
us that he had accountants as his neighbours, on both sides.

Captain Thomas Junior was, like Captain Thomas Senior,
a Methodist Christian, well-versed in the power of words. In
Tuckingmill, he proclaimed to those assembled at this public
meeting in 1864, "*there is a sufficiency of water*". Furthermore,
"*the inhabitants do not care about drainage*". "*This Act*", he
thundered, "*will vest in a Local Board power over drainage,
power over lighting, and power over water!*" The journalist
from the Royal Cornwall Gazette has faithfully recorded his
words and we can imagine Captain Thomas in full flow:

---

4   Conversion figures: £4,000 in 1846 = c.£518,000 today; £90,000 in
     1868 = c.£11.5 million today; £147,854 = c.£18.6 million today

"I ask all working men: Are you prepared to give up your rights into the hands of a few? Do you want to sell your liberties and all you possess? Is a pound of beef not a better thing for a working man than drainage or lighting?"

Immense applause resounded in the room after these last words sounded.

And then, this man of God concluded:

"As to health, we must consider not merely what is right, but what we can afford. There has been a great increase in local taxation in this parish of Camborne within the past few years and it is driving many a good working man out of the district."

He did not specify which *'good working men'* he was referencing, but it seems they were the ones who earned enough to be subject to paying rates, the local form of taxation. Such working men were not miners.

Captain James Rowe agreed, stating firmly that since most of the inhabitants earned their living by mining, the rate of mortality must necessarily be high.

The meeting was, in the words of the reporter, *'on the whole, a very noisy and irregular one.'*

Two very different visions of the social and economic landscape were colliding. Mr. E. Burgess responded with some passion to Captain Thomas, advising that it was the duty of the few who enjoyed advantages in life to concern themselves with the welfare of the masses of working people. The moral and physical welfare of a community depended upon an adequate supply of good water. The costs of securing such a supply would be trifling. The public meeting resounded with cries of "*Hear, hear!*" But a significant minority were of a different mind.

The structure of feeling, to use Raymond Williams's insightful phrase, was beginning to change in Victorian society. Or more tellingly, we can say that there were competing structures of feeling, rival ways of making sense of that changing world. Imagine, as Williams does, that we are visitors, guests from a different generation making sense of the culture of the period, made manifest in the words and actions of the members of those past communities. We are, at this public meeting in 1864, witnessing a clash between two such competing structures of feeling – and that conflict continues in similar ways to this day.

Reform was in the air, but then it had been for over fifty years – men and women were always seeking, in the name of efficiency as well as morality, to put right the glaring wrongs that arose from the unregulated pursuit of profit. This, after all, was a country that proclaimed itself to be Christian in belief and practice. Mr. Hutchinson, a prominent voice at the meeting, pointed out that a good deal of the water drunk in Camborne contained 'vegetable matter', so that those who drank it were constantly taking poison. Didn't this clearly require action? he implored. It was clear by his reference to shallow privies located nearby that Mr. Hutchinson was referring to human faeces, but such matters needed alluding to, not full-on naming in Victorian society. It was also Mr. Hutchinson who reminded the meeting that the solution could not be left to private enterprise since a private company would invest their money only with a view to profit. The Local Government Act of 1864 did not provide the opportunity for private profit. It was a measure designed to meet the needs of the many, not line the pockets of the few.

Industrialisation had led to the growth of towns that accompanied the exponential rise in population in Great Britain, from 10.5 million in 1801 to 16.8 million in 1851 and then to 30.5 million in 1901. Great wealth was created for some – and misery and death for so many. My own doctoral research (*Drink in Victorian Norwich,* U.E.A. 2003) has established that the working class majority in Norwich, as in all other urban centres, depended upon urban elites, the property owners, having the private conscience and the political will to address the degrading and unsanitary conditions in which most citizens lived in this new world of an ever-expanding population. In these circumstances, each central government commission and report from Westminster and each piece of public health legislation, albeit permissive rather than mandatory, was a lifeline for the masses. Such measures provided further opportunities for a change in outlook, a shift from one structure of feeling to another.

I am the twenty-first-century historian who has had access to clean water all his life. So too did my parents, my grandparents most likely did, my great-grandparents most certainly did not. Today, in the winter of 2022, I received a communication from WaterAid which shared the message from a field officer that in her country of Zambia, over forty per cent of people don't have clean water. In the developing world, the matter of clean water remains a problem. In our country, it took well over a century to get the better of the vested interests that prevented a solution. Here is Friedrich

Engels concluding his epic work, *The Condition of the Working Class in England in 1844*:

'On re-reading my description (of the Old Town of Manchester)… I must admit that… it is by far not nearly strong enough… to convey vividly the filth, ruination, and uninhabitableness, the defiance of every consideration of cleanliness, ventilation, and health that characterise the construction of this district, which contains at least twenty to thirty thousand inhabitants. And such a district exists in the very centre of the second city of England, the most important factory town in the world.'

My research established that despite the passing of an Act for the Better Sewering of Norwich in 1867 and the appointment of a first Medical Officer of Health in 1873, the city had to wait until the twentieth century and wholesale schemes of slum clearance in the 1920s before anything like a satisfactory system was to emerge. Likewise, the mining community of Camborne faced medical problems that were systemic and chronic throughout the Victorian period and beyond. There is further evidence in the section below, 'The Poor Man at His Gate'. Such issues remain endemic in a capitalist industrialising society for as long as profit is more valued than people, the pursuit of greater personal wealth more prized than the health and even life of others.

And now, after the scene-setting, it is time to turn back to the source material on page five and consider the matter of drink. Joseph Henry Thomas was sent to prison for twenty-eight days for being drunk and disorderly, and assaulting the

Looking from Dolcoath Mine northwards towards Redruth c.1890 (an unusually smoke-free day).[5]

police constable on the beat who intervened. Nothing out of the ordinary there. Victorian social cohesion depended to a significant degree on drink, as I argued in *Drink in Victorian Norwich*. Those who held power, within Camborne and elsewhere, were able to use working class dependence on the consumption of beer to maintain social order and control. As the population grew in urban centres across the land, so too did the supply of alcoholic drink – and the need and opportunity to police the drinking. In a later section (see below, pp.98-125), I will take you into a remarkable story, set in Camborne, describing how the social control exercised through the local police force backfired and produced the 1873 Camborne riots. Sufficient now to say that one of Camborne's public houses was renamed after the event as 'The Red Jackets' – testimony to the arrival of troops.

The working classes needed their public houses and beer-houses. They made their meaning in life in response to poverty, lack of education, and unhealthy living and

5   Source: Wikipedia

working conditions. Inadequate sanitation and water supply problems meant that beer answered a dietary need for a liquid that was safe to drink in a society where an alternative such as tea only became affordable and acceptable to increasing numbers later in the century. Depressant comfort came directly from their consumption of alcoholic drink. The ambience of their drinking places brought further social comforts. Poor Joseph Henry Thomas unfortunately got carried away in his search for solace – perhaps it was pay day – and paid the price.

Yet there were splits in society over the issue of drink – divisions within both the elite and the working classes. The Temperance Movement developed because of the challenge to traditional Christian ethics presented by the excessive consumption of drink in the new urban context created by the Industrial Revolution. For many supporters of Temperance within the elite, the sin of excessive drinking provided the explanation for the poverty and lack of virtue they identified within the working class. Joseph Henry Thomas was a reprobate who needed to be made an example of. The punishment had to fit the crime. Those who had power could determine when and how the lower orders drank their alcohol, even as the upper and middle orders in general escaped any public scrutiny or consequence of their own possible addiction to the licensed drug of alcohol.

For some within the working class of Camborne, as elsewhere, the attraction of temperance or abstinence went hand-in-glove with the appeal of the chapel. Not all the working class depended for their comfort and sustenance on the legal drug of alcohol. Some avoided it. Non-conforming churches such as Methodism offered an alternative comfort and meaning to that provided by the glass of alcohol. The love of God promised a graced life in the hereafter, as well as the love of neighbours within a church community. Deep down in the darkness of the mine shaft and its tunnels, the grace that came through being a man of God mattered.

Whether comfort was found in the bar or the chapel, the working classes shared a need to make sense of the difficult living and working conditions in which they found themselves and over which, in this Victorian period, they had little control. Men went underground to mine when work was on offer because they had little choice. Growing up in a mining community shapes horizons. What else was there? In fact, the human spirit to endure and seek alternatives did burn bright in Camborne, as in the rest of Cornwall. When the mine owners and other adventurers decided that the market price of copper or tin had fallen too low for the mine to make a profit, thousands of the miners who had then been laid off made their plans and emigrated with their families to the far-flung corners of the globe, such as Australia, South America, the USA, and parts of Asia. Wherever there were metallic ore mines, there were Cornish emigrants – 'Cousin Jacks', as they were known by the relatives left behind – attempting to carve out a new life. But for those many Cornish miners who did not emigrate, the cycle of employment and redundancy was the recurring feature of their usually short working lives.

How many miners made that momentous decision to leave the land in which they were born and travel, many with their families, across thousands of miles by sea to a foreign country in search of work? *The Tavistock Gazette* on Friday 10 May 1867, citing the *Cornish Telegraph*, recorded under the headline '*Knocked Mines and Exiled Miners*' that:

'...*nearly 300 mines are now idle throughout Cornwall and Devonshire... and that the following list is a close approximation to the real numbers of the miners who have emigrated: -*

'*From Tavistock and Ashburton Districts 691*

'*Liskeard 100*

'*St Austell and St Blazey 275*

'*Redruth and St Agnes 300*

'*Camborne 150*

'*Hayle 550*

'*St Ives and Lelant 150*

'*St Just 600*

'*Helston and Wendron 100*

'*Marazion and St Erth 450*

'*Total: 3,366*

'*These are all able-bodied men, and the most skilled and most active of the mining population. The wives and families who have accompanied them are not reckoned in the above tables, but would swell up the list very much. Within the past few months the tide of emigration has been, in most districts, comparatively, on a very small scale, and in some localities it has almost ceased, but how long before this will recommence or stop depends much upon the state of trade for the next few weeks.*'

Five years later, *The Redruth Times* and *Camborne Advertiser*, on Friday 17 May 1872, recorded under the headline '*Emigration of miners*':

'*A large number of Cornish miners have already emigrated and a still larger number are preparing to go.*

Now, such men are skilled hands, most of them active, experienced, and in the prime of life, and therefor this departure from England cannot but result in a loss to the country. Notwithstanding their recently improved conditions and prospects, they are attracted by the reports received of higher wages abroad, and they go.'

Historians can be grateful for the Victorian love affair with statistics. Discovering the figures for emigration in 1867 is not only valuable as an indicator of the scale of movement overseas, but it also serves to widen the perspective, to place Camborne within its Cornish context, and to show the scale of mining in Cornwall. This county, a place renowned for its land- and seascapes, and now so dependent on tourism, is riddled with shafts and tunnels underground where men were maimed and died.

***

When men first went underground to mine, they did so with hammers and chisels and gunpowder. In the late 1870s, a new tool was developed, manufactured, and soon used in the mines of Cornwall. It was the compressed air power drill. And this development brings us to the tragedy of James Mager, as revealed in the second newspaper source from 1889, the young miner who collapsed and died, earning a wage working on the surface with the women and other men too ill to work underground anymore. What had happened to James Mager, fathoms deep underground, that now left his body reduced to a blood-soaked corpse and a widow and child dependent on charity?

Gustavus Basset, also known by the titles of Lord de Dunstanville and Chief of the Mineral Lords, who controlled the Tehidy estate from his succession in 1870 to his death in 1888, played his part in the chain of events that led to James Mager's death. As Michael Tangye records, Gustavus Basset was 'largely responsible for introducing the rock drill into Cornwall, donating £500 towards the first experiment at Carn Brea Mine' in the late 1870s. There was much money to be made in this remarkably more efficient way of drilling using compressed air to power the drill.[6]

There is a succinct explanation in J.A. Buckley's *The Cornish Mining Industry – A Brief History* (1992/2002, pp.35-41) of what was going on underground in Cornwall and in the wider world beyond in the nineteenth century. It throws much light on how the Basset family became so rich – and most likely why James Mager died. By the mid-nineteenth century, the extraction of copper that had underpinned the success of Cornish mining for two hundred years was on the wane: 'copper lodes were being exhausted at a faster rate than fresh ones were discovered, and new, enormously rich discoveries of copper were being found in America and elsewhere.'

The Williams family, who had made a fortune from copper smelting, now moved their money from copper mining into tin mining, becoming principal shareholders in the Dolcoath mine which lay under the land owned by the Basset family. Tin-bearing lodes lay under the copper zones. The mine shafts had to go deeper.

The manager of Dolcoath, as we have noted already, was Charles Thomas Senior. He realised, as the copper seams

---

6   £500 in late 1870s = c.£60,250 today

gave out, that there were increases in the quantity of tin ore to be found in the mine's deeper workings. His reports persuaded the Basset family and the adventurers, those who were helping finance the mining enterprise, to sink deeper shafts. J.A. Buckley writes:

'Dolcoath Main Lode is one of the wonders of Cornish mining, extending for a mile east of the Great Crosscourse, being worked to depths up to 3000 ft from surface and over 60 ft wide in places. It has parallel branches that are 100 ft across. This pattern, although not on the same scale, was repeated in the mines around Dolcoath... [such as] Carn Brea, Cooks Kitchen, East Pool and South Wheal Crofty.'

The Basset family, lords of the manor at Tehidy, were sitting on a fortune, and all they needed, or so it must have seemed to them, were the men to go underground and drill and blast their way deeper and deeper, branching out horizontally at each new level. But for the men what a toll of their health it took to even get to the lowest and furthest depths. Hamilton Jenkin (1927/2004) calculated that in the mid-nineteenth century:

'...a Cornish miner... as often or not, walked five or six miles across rough country, at all hours of the day and night, to reach his work, climbed down 200 fathoms of ladders, and after working an eight-hour core underground, repeated the climb to surface and the walk home across the moors to his cottage across the moors.

'In mines such as Wheal Vor, Dolcoath, Cook's Kitchen, Gwennap United, and Fowey Consols, all of which were close on 300 fathoms deep, "it takes the men three-quarters of an hour to descend and an hour and a quarter to ascend the perpendicular ladders to and from their work," wrote G. Henwood in 1854.'

Even when a man-engine replaced the ladders, it still took time to reach the workings and begin the shift. The ride to the bottom of the shaft at Levant, near St Just, using the mine engine installed in 1857 (and which suffered a catastrophic break in 1919 that led to the deaths of thirty-one men – see below, pp.163-186) took half an hour, followed by a walk out under the sea which could be a further mile and another half an hour.

If the Bassets and other mine owners, and the adventurers who helped finance them, were oblivious to the life-shortening conditions underground, they were also blind to the perils of their dependence on a commodity whose value was and is determined by global market conditions.

Since the Bronze Age (bronze is an alloy of tin and copper), tin had been found on the surface in the alluvial deposits of rivers and their flood plains in Cornwall. It is a county shaped by the granite rock under its surface, which contains the lodes of cassiterite that carry the deposits of tin ore. Only when these alluvial areas had been stripped bare did men need to mine under the surface. One of the reasons why the Romans came to Britain and stayed was tin. The Latin for tin is *stennum*; the home where my wife and I live is in the valley where the river Stennack flows, now for the most part under the pavement and road, down to the harbour and bay at St Ives. Water and tin had a close connection in Cornwall.

By the mid-nineteenth century, global market conditions began to work against the interests of Cornish tin mining underground. The value of extensive alluvial deposits of tin in Malaya had been recognised and streaming this ore had begun, leading to the price crash of the 1840s that closed many tin mines in Cornwall. However, when the Malaysian territories suffered a period of anarchy and piracy in the 1860s, which continued into the 1870s, tin production dropped substantially. Consequently, the price of tin rocketed, as Buckley notes, 'reaching a record £153 a ton and [Cornish] tin mines opened, re-opened and expanded.'

But then came another consequence of being in an international marketplace. Britain was an imperial power in the nineteenth century. Its position as the wealthiest nation on the planet had been secured, in part, by its control of the seas. Here is Buckley again:

'The Royal Navy intervened in Malaya to restore order and, inevitably, eastern production resumed and the price collapsed once again. By 1874 it was down to £56 a ton and most of the re-opened mines closed. It bottomed in 1878 at an unbelievable £35 a ton. By that time discoveries of tin in Australia and Tasmania contributed to world production; ironically it was Cornishmen who discovered it there and Cornishmen who rushed to exploit it. The next twenty years were among the most depressing in the long history of Cornish mining. In 1896 the price had dropped again to £64.'[7]

---

7   £153 a ton = c.£20,500 today; £56 a ton in 1874 = c.£7,504 today; £35 a ton in 1878 = c.£4,445 today; £64 a ton in 1896 = c.£9,088

What twists and turns there have been in this story of tin mining in a capitalist global economy. The Cornish miners who risked their lives to feed themselves and their families could find themselves out of a job because the price of tin was falling on the London market due to events elsewhere in a world that was shaped by their British government's actions. Those same miners, some with their families, might then be among those who took the option of emigration to salvage some meaning and earn a living. And they, as successful 'Cousin Jacks', would then play their part in keeping down the international price of tin.

There was yet another reason why drilling and blasting was not the panacea to all ills, the pathway to a cornucopia. The new rock drills proved highly efficient tools, but they were also instruments of death. The miners had a name for them: widow-makers.

Take yourself down to the rock face, let's say 1000 feet below ground. For a moment, consider all the drilling and blasting that has gone on, through one of the hardest rocks in

the world, granite, to get to such a depth in the pursuit of profit. Think about how many years it has taken for this shaft to be sunk to this point – and how many men it has taken.

Stoping at the 170 level in
East Pool Mine, Illogan,
photographed by J.C. Burrows

in 1893. The miner on the left is using a pick while to his right two pares are boring holes for blasting. Pares refers to a small gang of men, often three as here, with two men wielding hammers and one turning the drill.[8]

Remarkably, we have a powerful visual aid to help our imagination. J.C. Burrows was a Victorian photographer whose innovative use of flashlight in the 1880s and onwards made it possible to capture the reality of mining lives. This group of three men in the image above are engaged in one of the early acts of stoping, the process of mining the tin-rich lode. Their aim was to extract the narrow strip of ore-bearing rock whilst removing as little as possible of the barren rock on either side. They worked together to drill a series of holes. Then explosives were inserted in the holes and the rock was blasted away.

Since the introduction of gunpowder in the late seventeenth century, all shot holes had been hand-drilled. According to Buckley, three men in an underground stope could expect to drill two four-foot holes in a shift. Then, in the 1860s, a technological breakthrough began to change the world of mining. F.B. Doering designed a compressed air rock-boring machine which had limited success, but others improved on the idea and by 1878 the 'Barrow Rock Drill', patented by Cornishmen in Barrow-in-Furness, was introduced into the working of Dolcoath Mine, with the financial support of Gustavus Basset. Weighing only 120 lbs and easily manoeuvrable for drilling at various angles, it was very efficient and advanced a level much faster.

---

8   Source: www.imagearchive.royalcornwallmuseum.org.uk

The rock drill in the hands of two miners at the 375 level in Dolcoath Mine, Camborne. This image was taken by JC Burrows in March 1904.[9]

This invention, nevertheless, was a lethal killing machine that led not only to the possibility of more profit but also to increased mortality. Dust from drilling had been a health-hazard for miners before the arrival of the new rock drill, but now the likes of James Mager, and so many others, died prematurely because their lungs were peppered with microscopic fragments of rock which they inhaled as they drilled. The medical term for this industrial injury is silicosis.

Silicosis is an incurable lung disease caused by inhaling dust that contains free crystalline silica. Silicosis is the result of the body's response to the presence of the silica dust in the lung. Silica dust particles are tiny and reach deep into

---

9   Source: www.imagearchive.royalcornwallmuseum.org.uk

the lungs as far as the alveoli. These are the tiny sacs which are the final termini in the airways of the lungs where the walls are only one cell thick. Here, the natural magic occurs which allows the exchange of gases between the lungs and the blood stream.

The dust particles which land on such surfaces as the alveoli are removed by white blood cells known as macrophages. However, the particles of free crystalline silica cause the macrophages to break open, leaving scar-like patches on the surface. When many of these 'scars' form, the alveolar surface becomes less elastic. This effect, in turn, reduces the transfer of gases and can then lead to health problems ranging from shortness of breath to a slow, agonising death due to lack of oxygen. The victim is literally suffocating internally.

There are three major types of silicosis: acute, chronic, and extended. Acute silicosis occurs after a few months or up to two years of exposure to extremely high concentrations. For some, death may quickly follow. Chronic silicosis occurs after fifteen to twenty years of moderate to low exposures. In the later stages, the worker may experience fatigue, extreme shortness of breath, chest pain, or respiratory failure, potentially leading to death. Accelerated silicosis is quicker than chronic silicosis and can be detected after five to ten years of high exposure. Symptoms include severe shortness of breath, weakness, and weight loss, again with the risk of death.

Interestingly, my science and medical advisor in the USA, Dr. Howard Pue, has informed me in April 2022 that researchers are now linking silica dust directly to black lung disease, also known as progressive massive fibrosis, among coal miners. It is estimated that silica is around twenty times more toxic than coal dust. The exposure to silica has come from miners now cutting into sandstone as they mine coal, a practice which has become more common in recent decades as larger coal deposits were exhausted in Appalachia. As the mining machines operate, the quartz in the sandstone turns into sharp silica particles that are easily inhaled and can lodge in the lungs permanently.

Plus ca change! It seems there are none so blind as those who are focused on making a profit. Appalachian coal miners in the twenty-first century inhaling silica are contracting the same kind of terminal illness as those people mining tin and copper in the nineteenth and twentieth centuries who were also inhaling silica.

Precise medical understanding based on scientific research was not available in the late-nineteenth century, but the miners and their employers knew that they faced a new problem. Very soon, Cornish firms – notably R. Stephens & Son and Holman Bros – began to manufacture modified machines that were equipped with a water line carrying water through the drill steel to the face to dampen down the dust and limit the damage from inhalation. But the hazard had not been eliminated and many working places, as Buckley points out, still lacked piped water for such use. Moreover, the water jets were not welcomed by the miners. They ended up drenched and the high humidity they already endured working at deep levels became even more intense and unbearable. They disconnected the water supplies and worked without the jets. This we know thanks to S.W. Sturdy's doctoral thesis (1971), cited by E.S. Proctor in an article – 'The health of the Cornish tin miner 1840-1914' – published in the *Journal of the Royal Society of Medicine* (volume 92, November 1999). This article I use below and will reference again in my section 'The Poor Man at his Gate'.

We cannot be certain whether James Mager was a victim of rock drilling, but it seems likely. Tin miners were prone to many different diseases because of working in such hot, damp, and dusty conditions underground. The deeper the mine was drilled, the worse the conditions became. The 1842 Royal Commission into the employment of children in mines had shown: '...for the first time the abundance of lung disease amongst Cornish miners and found it to be the reason for the excessive mortality first recorded in 1840 by Mr. Blee of the Royal Cornwall Polytechnic Society.'

By 1864, Dr. William Farr of the Registrar General's Office had investigated adult Cornish miners' ill health and concluded that Cornish miners had an excess mortality that was mainly attributable to respiratory organ disease, commonly known then as miners' phthisis. Phthisis is an archaic medical term that comes from a Greek root meaning 'a dwindling or wasting away', as in the case and manner of Mimi, the heroine and victim of tuberculosis, in Puccini's 1896 opera *La bohème*.

James Mager, too, was a victim of phthisis, respiratory organ disease. He died because of his work underground.

Rest in peace, James Mager.

***

And so, to the third source taken from that newspaper, giving details of a recent Camborne concert where there was 'a large attendance.' Who were these people? I have found no source which provides an answer, but the question does raise the issue of the nature of Camborne society. My social division of Camborne people is three-fold, a little crude, but I think such a move has obvious meaning and justification. There was a life as understood by the likes of those who lived in the mansion at Tehidy; such upper class people comprised around two per cent of the population in the Victorian era. There was a life for those I group as the middle class of Camborne; such people comprised around fifteen per cent of the national population. And then there was a life for the working class of Camborne; such people comprised most of the national population - around eighty-three per cent. These percentage figures are based on census analysis and serve as approximate calculations, but they are a plausible guide to understanding the nature of Victorian society in general and the world of Camborne in particular.

The Camborne concert referred to in the newspaper piece was a meeting of the middle class, for the most part. However, to understand more about what brought such a large gathering together, we need to start at the great house of Tehidy.

There, the style associated with an elite family the equal of any in the land continued to be nurtured through the coffers of the Basset fortune. Michael Tangye (2002) reports from material in the county record office that back in 1773, in the decade when the great house took on its Georgian appearance, Richard Radford, of Exeter, stayed at Tehidy for eleven weeks 'by Francis Basset's order, teaching his servants Paul Seager and Joseph Whitaker to blow a French Horn.' Playing and listening to music, together with the support of such arts, were critical to the statement of style that every great family needed to make in their own house, whether in London or in Cornwall. Whatever might be lacking in musical proficiency could be bought.

Within the great house, the harpsichord was now replaced by a large organ and a pianoforte. When Thomas Staniforth, a successful Liverpool banker, visited Tehidy in 1800, he recorded in his diary that: '...*our entertainment was handsome and the wines such as did credit to his Lordship's taste... his Lordship showed us some curious specimens of copper ore and Miss Basset play'd on the pianoforte...*'

Over time, there would have been other Miss Bassets displaying their musical accomplishments.

The library in the first decade of the twentieth century.[10]

---

10   Source: www.imagearchive.royalcornwallmuseum.org.uk

As for the organ, it was on the right-hand side of the hall, a statement of grandeur seen on entry into the house.

The hall at Tehidy in the first decade of the twentieth century. The grand organ is just visible on the right.[11]

Can even musical instruments experience hubris? Or simply the joys of a different and less regulated life? Here are the words of Mr. Fred Hayes, aged 83 in 1984, describing Tehidy as he remembered it and recorded by Michael Tangye:

'We youngsters were overawed by the inside of the mansion. The family were usually away, but I was friendly with the Governess and was allowed to

---

11 Source: www.imagearchive.royalcornwallmuseum.org.uk

wander around. There were tall pillars in the front hall and the great organ was on the righthand side. This was sold to the Skating Rink at Camborne when the Bassets eventually left.'

There is such a distance between the fate of that organ in a twentieth century Camborne skating rink and the world of Sir Francis Basset, Lord de Dunstanville (1757-1835) whose memorial rested on a wall in Illogan church until it was pulled down in 1845. Here, in this Illogan church, the Basset family worshipped and were, eventually, buried. Each Sunday morning, when they were in residence, the Basset coach set out from the great house and made its way across the park to the East Lodge, and on to the church. The staff followed them on foot. Inside the church, everyone had their due position in the hierarchy of deference. In 1788, Sir Francis introduced 'a choir of singers accompanied by a bassoon, who occupied a small gallery at the west end', according to the churchwarden's accounts. The good Lord was praised by the making of music.

When the last lord of the manor, Arthur Basset, married Miss Rebecca Harriet Buller Trelawney in 1898 at Truro Cathedral, the elite of Cornwall were present, as they still were when the procession of carriages had made their way south after the service through the county to the reception at Tehidy. The newly married couple and their families finally entered the mansion to the strains of Mendelssohn's 'Wedding March' resounding from the great organ in the hall. Music was made to fill the air in praise of the Almighty and his wondrous ways. The rich man in his great house could also bask in the beauty of that sound and the knowledge that his wealth was making all this possible. Little did he and his family know what fate had in store.

Meanwhile, those lower down the social hierarchy continued to imitate those above them. For very many members of the middle class, being respectable meant being seen attending a place of worship, an Anglican church or Methodist chapel. And for very many, an association with the world of music was another key marker of respectability. As we know from the third source, there was a 'large attendance' at the Pengegon Wesleyan chapel in November 1889, at the concert given by the chapel choir and the Philharmonic band, all under the baton of Mr. F. Miller with five named singers. This would have been another evening to remember, an occasion when those present, making music or listening, knew they were indeed in some respects like those who lived in the grand house at Tehidy.

One of the twists of history is that by the end of the second decade of the twenty-first century, due to the death of the mining industry in Camborne in the second half of the twentieth century, Pengegon had become the most health-deprived area in Cornwall and the second most deprived in income. But as the nineteenth century ended, the Pengegon district in Camborne was largely the place of residence for respectable, middle class families.

THE RICH MAN IN
HIS CASTLE

Sources:
Mrs. C.F. Alexander, 'Hymns for Little Children'
(1848), 'All Things Bright and Beautiful', v.3:

> The rich man in his castle,
> The poor man at his gate,
> God made them, high or lowly,
> And ordered their estate.
> *All things bright and beautiful,*
> *All creatures great and small,*
> *All things wise and wonderful,*
> *The Lord God made them all.*

**Michael Tangye, *Tehidy and the Bassets – the Rise and Fall
of a Great Cornish Family* (1984/2002, Truran):**

Tangye, page forty-two, quoting from the *Royal
Cornwall Gazette*, 8th May 1802, on the occasion
of the coming of age at twenty-one years of the

Honourable Miss Frances Basset, only child of Lord de Dunstanville: 'The [church] bells of Camborne and Illogan pealed forth at daybreak. For the poor of each parish was a large ox, fattened for the event, 27 bushels of wheat, and one hogshead of beer.'

Tangye, pages forty-four to forty-five, quoting from the *Western Morning News*, 15th February 1933, in which Sir Ian Hamilton recorded his recollections of Tehidy and John Francis Basset:

'The youngest sister of my mother… married the most extraordinary being I have ever met – Francis Basset was his name. As a child I was always told he was the fifth richest commoner in England, and daresay this may have been true. One of his many sources of wealth was the Dolcoath tin mine… (he) lived in a splendid Mansion called Tehidy… and the wrought iron balconies around the first storey of the house had intertwined in gold the initials of my Uncle Francis and Aunt Emily. They brought over from Italy… seven or eight Italian artists, who painted the ceilings with all sorts of pictures… But of all these marvels the strangest was my uncle himself. He had long hair and a very curly yellow beard. He spoke in short sentences, and between each sentence said in a resounding rumbling sort of voice, either 'Ta-ra-rum' or 'Ta-ra-ra-rum'. They had a very fine house in Charles Street, London. My aunt always drove in a chariot with a bewigged coachman and two powdered footmen hanging on behind. My uncle had a magnificent deer forest in Scotland, and he drove me up to it. Such people have now ceased to exist for at least 70 years.'

I can remember singing the hymn 'All Things Bright and Beautiful' when I was a kid at primary school. Back in the 1950s, the third verse, as printed above, was sung with as much relish as the other verses. However, a decade later this trace of a moribund structure of feeling had vanished from direct view. My 1966 copy of *Songs of Praise* contains the hymn, but the third verse has disappeared.

When I sang these words at my junior school, no doubt tunelessly, I was, without knowing it, internalising the message that we are who we are because we are all part of a plan decreed by the Good Lord. This plan had remarkable overlaps with a world finely tuned to the interests of those who held wealth and power in the nation. My child voice was proclaiming that there is an order in society that must be upheld. We must trust in Divine Providence, and all will be well. We must follow those who know best, those who have been born to lead and govern us.

Mrs. Alexander, the writer of this hymn, had a privileged Protestant Anglo-Irish background. She had to make sense of an Irish famine caused by a disease in the staple food of the potato. Starvation and death were scything their way through the largely Catholic lower orders in Ireland between 1845 and 1852. It is estimated that one million Irish died because of the famine, another million emigrated; the Irish population declined by nearly twenty-five per cent.

All the while, the British government in Westminster did very little to help. Best to draw a line under all that suffering and repeat a deeply conservative message, reinforced by a theology which has God in control of whatever happens. Those who had wealth and power were let off the hook and the pursuit of profit continued as the primary directive.

It was not just the poor's estate that was being ordered, it was their fate.

***

Michael Tangye, the Camborne local historian and my source for much detail about the owners of Tehidy, notes that Arthur Basset had 'inherited a degree of public ill will, created by his father, Gustavus.' He continues:

> 'In 1882, Gustavus, being confined to a Bath Chair, had lawn-like paths created above Spratting (Basset) Cove along which he was pushed by a servant. A notice was erected threatening prosecution to those who picnicked on this area of cliff on which miners and their families had traditionally spent their leisure. Conybeare MP, the radical champion of the miners, personally removed the sign' [presumably after his election as the MP in 1885]. (Tangye cites the *West Briton*, 29.10.1888, as his source.)

Charles Augustus Vansittart Conybeare (1853-1919) was an English barrister who became a radical politician and sat in the House of Commons as a Member of Parliament from 1885 to 1895. He was elected as the MP for Camborne in 1885 and only then took the Liberal whip. Re-elected in 1886, he held the seat until 1895 and was nicknamed the 'Miners' Friend'. Charles Conybeare will feature again in the section titled 'The Poor Man at his Gate'.

Tangye explains that Gustavus Basset, as an officer in the Crimean War (1849-52), suffered frost bite which later led to paralysis of his lower limbs, hence his need for a bath chair by 1882. Prior to that, it seems he was driven around the estate 'in a small carriage, drawn by a pony, with an attendant walking by his side.' A degree of deference towards the Basset family as lords of the manor may be evident in the report from Tangye, citing the *West Briton* and the *Cornubian* in 1888, that:

'A kind man, he [Gustavus] frequently took the aged Illogan postman to the post-office at Camborne and returned him to the village. He also bore gifts for the patients when attending weekly meetings at the Miners' Hospital.'

If, indeed, he did show such kindness as an act of *noblesse oblige*, his character had other sides. It was, after all, Gustavus Basset who was largely responsible for introducing the rock drill into Cornwall. Tangye notes that:

'In 1883, Gustavus shattered the long amicable relationship with the Adventurers of Dolcoath Mine. He advised the sinking of a new shaft, demanding that unless they agreed, £40,000 would have to be paid to him when the new lease was taken up. He finally succeeded in extracting £25,000 at a time when local mines were struggling to survive' (Tangye again cites the *West Briton* and the *Cornubian*).[12]

---

12 £40,000 in 1883 = c.£5.2 million today; £25,000 = c.£3.25 million today

His son, Arthur Basset, continued this path of exploitation, a policy which damaged the financial interests of other members of the urban elite. He claimed thousands of pounds for 'damaged lands' from both the Dolcoath mine company and from the South Frances mine company prior to its amalgamation with Wheal Basset in 1895. Charles Conybeare voiced an opinion of both miners and adventurers when the MP stated: 'The grasping policy of the vampire Lord is a tradition of the office' (Tangye cites the *Cornubian*, 29.9.1895).

It was clear that as the end of the century approached, the feudal nature of Camborne society, evident in the source extract from the *Royal Cornwall Gazette* in 1802, was under strain. Yet, it is remarkable how unaware those in the big house at Tehidy might have been of such a fundamental change. Tangye records the words of an octogenarian from Illogan, within the Camborne district, who voiced this memory in 1982, reflecting on the long-established tradition of the Christmas Eve charity distribution at the Tehidy estate during Arthur Basset's time as lord of the manor:

'Every Christmas Eve I used to go to the gate of the lodge and sit in a wicker chair watching the widows of miners who had died in the mines, pass up the drive to the mansion. They were given an article of their choice – either a coat, blanket, or a hundred weight of coal, which they trundled home in a barrow. They thought the Bassets were wonderful. They'd forgotten their husbands had died at thirty years of age for their benefit!'

Life in Tehidy continued much as it always had, even as Arthur Basset was losing the family fortune gambling on the horses. We have seen (above, page seven) how John Francis Basset was responsible for the rebuild of the family house at Tehidy between 1861 and 1863. Citing the *West Briton*, Tangye records that during 1860-61 John Francis Basset's dues from Dolcoath and other Basset mines yielded an income of £20,000 a year. Beyond the manor of Tehidy he owned most of Perranarworthal, part of St Gluvias, and property in Meneage, Greenback Terrace and a hotel in Falmouth. There were other properties in Falmouth owned on lease. Further valuable property was held at Tywardreath and a large ancestral estate and mansion in the parish of Whitstone in north Cornwall. He also held the valuable church livings of Camborne, Illogan, Redruth, Bodmin, and West Buckland. It was money from mining and land that paid for the £150,000 rebuild of Tehidy.[13]

Religious observance played a key part in the continuation of life at Tehidy. The Bassets and the local Anglican church went together like a horse and carriage. This harmony provided a living witness to the power and authority underpinning the notion that 'God made them high or lowly, and ordered their estate.' When the old church in Illogan had become too small and dilapidated, it was pulled down in 1845 and a new church built. The memorials and monuments to the Bassets and their stewards were carefully replaced within the new church, which opened for worship in 1846 and now included a fine bust of Francis Basset, Lord de Dunstanville (1757-1835), created by the Royal Academy

---

13   £20,000 in 1860 = c.£2.6 million today; £150,000 = c.£19.5 million today

sculptor Sir Richard Westacott. The Basset vault remained outside in its original position near the old tower that had been saved as a daymark for shipping. A new Basset pew of oak was erected in the north aisle.

Michael Tangye provides eye-witness accounts from local men and women as they recalled seeing, in their childhood, Arthur Basset with his wife Rebecca and daughter Patience attend this Victorian Illogan church:

'The late Mrs. Maud Brown, aged 78 years in 1982, stated: "I was confirmed in Illogan church in 1912, the same time as Miss Patience. The Bassets attended in a carriage and pair with a footman and driver. They had a special pew with tall wooden sides so that we only saw the tops of their heads when they stood up to sing a hymn."

'The late Miss M. Luke remembered: "At this time the Tehidy servants would ride to church in a large waggonette or brake, drawn by horses, and later replaced by a motorcoach. They seemed to be a fair congregation on their own."

'Mr. Fred Haines, aged 83 years in 1984, recalled: "Until Squire Arthur Basset bought his cars he went to church in a horse-drawn carriage. There were stables around three sides of the stable square and the east side was then converted to garages. He had about six cars, his first one was AF1. The limousine was a Hodgekiss. The interior smelt of beautiful leather. There were also two large Daimler shooting brakes, chain driven, for collecting guests and their luggage from Camborne station when they held large house parties. Arthur Everett was the chauffeur. He took the Bassets into Camborne and collected shopping. Squire Basset came to church in the Hodgekiss and the servants travelled in the Daimler which had seats on each side."

'Mrs. C. Chappell, aged 83 years when interviewed, had similar memories: "The fourteen servants from the mansion came in a 14-seater vehicle. There were two huge stoves in the church and one of them was in the Basset pew. Each held about half a cwt of coal. The servants had their own pew. The church was lit by oil lamps in those days. Mr. Basset always put a sovereign in the collection. Mrs Basset had a fine voice and every Christmas she stood by the organ and sang 'Nazareth'".

These people are not like us would have been one of the first thoughts to spring to mind when these two worlds met – the Basset family circle, with selected servants drawn into their orbit, on the one hand, and the rest of Camborne, working class and middle class, on the other.

Generations of Bassets of course lived the sporting life: hunting, fishing, and shooting. Arthur Basset was no exception. The ramparts of the Iron Age camp at Nance above the adjoining Illogan Woods provided, as Tangye notes, a perfect spot for pheasant shooting:

'One such event was reported in 1899: "Mr. Basset's shooting party had good sport last week. On Tuesday they killed 703 pheasants, on Wednesday 785 and on Thursday 1109. On two succeeding days they shot

four white pheasants, and one day four wild ducks"
(*West Briton*, 4.12.1899).

Tangye's research further established that as late as 1911, Arthur Basset ordered the creation of large pheasant pens and that, in 1915, the cost of raising a pheasant had been 3s 3d, cheaper than the 4s 6d in 1914.[14] Such pastimes were expensive. The Basset gamekeepers, of course, still patrolled the woods to protect game from poaching. Tangye's concluding comment is worth passing on in full: 'To the starving poor, the game provided a constant temptation, especially on viewing such senseless slaughter.'

There are, I suggest, links between the senseless slaughter of birds bred to be shot dead and the maiming and early death of miners, extracting tin for the benefit of the few. Those links, I believe, are part of a chain that extends to the killing fields in the Great War that saw the slaughter of 20 million between 1914 and 1918 – and such a chain continues to this day. More on those links as this idiosyncratic history book unfolds.

As we have noted already, Arthur Basset's obsession for horse racing, with its accompanying betting, proved his undoing. He returned from his honeymoon in 1898 with a magnificent horse, 'Trail', which he had purchased for 5,000 guineas and paraded it around the lawn at Tehidy before his wife and staff (*West Briton*, 10.2.1898).[15] His horses were kept in stables throughout England, including those at Tehidy. But by the time of the Great War (1914-18), Arthur Basset's fortune was evaporating in gambling debts. He was

14 3s 3d in 1915 = c.£25 today; 4s 6d in 1914 = c.£27 today

15 5,000 guineas in 1898 = c.£720,000 today

spending much of his time in London as a recruiting officer, organising the selection and dispatch of men to the killing fields of western Europe. There were fewer and fewer men left to work the Tehidy estate and the grounds deteriorated. Tangye quotes one of his aged eyewitnesses, remembering a visit by Squire Arthur Basset to his tenant-farming parents to tell them of his decision to sell their farm: 'He came and sat wearily on the step at the farmhouse door, and said to my father "I am sorry, but it's the horses you know".

The mansion was vacated in 1915, and in November 1916 the manor was sold, house by house, farm by farm. By 1917, the Tehidy woodlands were providing timber for the local mines. A thought-provoking twist, this – the timber residue from the now-dead Basset enterprise, which had for so long sucked capital from underground at such costs in ill health and death for the working class, now found its way underground to prop up further exploitation of those who extracted and processed tin.

THE POOR MAN AT HIS GATE – MINING COMMUNITIES SUFFERING FROM LACK OF SANITATION AND EXPLOITATION AT WORK

S ources:
The Cornish Telegraph – Thursday 24 February 1881:

The Health of the Camborne District
Mr. E.S. Angove, the medical officer, reported that… the death rate for the previous year [1880] was 24 per thousand. This is much higher than in the year 1879. The deaths among children under five years of age numbered 167, being at the rate of 11.1 per thousand. This excess of deaths is in a large measure due to the epidemic of whooping cough… There were thirty-eight deaths from this disease among children.

The district has also been visited with two outbreaks of typhoid fever, causing twelve deaths. The Newton epidemic I consider was brought about by the use of impure water from a stream which runs behind the Newton row of houses and which supplies the engine at South Tolcarne mine... We had a fresh attack of typhoid, unconnected with the Newton epidemic, in December. All those affected were employed in the Cook's Kitchen mines, and they resided in various parts of the district. All they had in common was the water used for drinking purposes in the mines, which was procured and kept in a large barrel. As soon as this circumstance had been discovered the authorities of the mine were communicated with; they at once had the barrel examined and finding that it contained a considerable amount of dirt, they had it thoroughly cleaned and have now arranged for water from the Camborne reservoir to be brought into the mines in pipes, so as to have a continuous and pure supply.

The number of deaths from diseases of the respiratory organs were not quite so numerous as in 1879. There were fifty-three deaths from bronchitis, pneumonia, and pleurisy. The deaths from phthisis were also less, being thirty-five as against forty-seven in 1879.

Anonymous, 'Ankylostomiasis: its cause, treatment, and prevention' in *Supplement to the Colliery Guardian*, London: The Colliery Guardian Company, 1905 (as cited in E.S. Proctor, 1999, *The health of the Cornish tin miner 1840-1914* in J.R. Soc. Med. 1999):

'The Royal Commission into the Health of Cornish Tin Miners... discovered that most of the current disease was due to an infection by the ankylostoma hookworm that had been brought to the mines by men who had worked in the tropics... Transmission was faecal-oral, and the epidemic was due to a lack of sanitation in the mines… However, it was the miners who were blamed for the disease, the commissioners judging that their dirty habits, not the lack of sanitation, were the cause of the outbreak.'

Captain W. Rutter, the manager of East Crofty, in 1864, giving evidence before the Royal Commission into the Condition of Mines:

Captain W. Rutter, the manager at East Crofty, was asked by the Commissioners what became of the club money after the mine was closed. He explained that he was very sorry to say that the adventurers devoted some of it to working the mine again after they decided to reopen it. Rutter exclaimed: 'I told the purser, then and there, tooth and nail, that they were taking the blood and bones of the men.'

One of the first fruits of my digital research in Cornish Victorian newspapers for references to Camborne and mining was the report in the *Royal Cornwall Gazette* of a public meeting concerned with public health and the inadequate drainage of sewers on Friday 12 August 1864 (see above, pp.10-17). I suggested in my analysis of this report that the mining community of Camborne faced medical problems that were systemic and chronic throughout the Victorian period and beyond. My further investigations have helped confirm that proposition. *The Cornish Telegraph* on Thursday 24 February 1881, as cited in the sources above, carried a full account of the report of Mr. E.S. Angove, the medical officer for Camborne, on the public health of the district, delivered at the meeting of the Camborne Local Board.

Local Boards, in effect local boards of health, had been instruments of local government since 1848 when they were set up by the national government in Westminster in response to the cholera epidemic of that year. Such Boards had the powers to control sewers, clean the streets, regulate local health risks such as slaughterhouses, and ensure a safe supply of water to the district. Some Boards were eventually merged with the corporations of municipal boroughs when they were established in 1873; those that remained, such as the Camborne Local Board, were merged with urban districts when they were created in 1894.

The report, and the exchanges that followed, are reproduced, *ad verbatim*, in the account. Some seventeen years have passed since that public meeting in 1864 where such matters were so hotly discussed and, in that period, Camborne has acquired an official – Mr. Angove – with a paid responsibility for the oversight of public health. Yet, there is still clear evidence for the continued existence of the two competing structures of feeling that were apparent in 1864.

Captain Charles Thomas Junior, the champion of the conservative view that those with wealth and power must consider 'not merely what is right, but what we can afford' (see above, p.15) is now, in 1881, fifty years old, still active in public life, and as ever resistant to social change. His voice carries weight, even if it is becoming a minority view. After Mr. Angove had made his report, which highlighted cases of whooping cough and typhoid, Captain Thomas weighed in:

"What does Mr. Angove call typhoid fever?"

"Typhoid fever is, I believe, generally understood to be typhoid fever," replied Mr. Angove.

Laughter broke out. Captain Thomas, undeterred, ploughed on.

"Perhaps so. But would you say a man has typhoid fever who had only been confined to his bed a few days? I have the names of men who were only away from work for a very short time."

"Will you tell me who they were?" responded Mr. Angove.

"One case is that of Dunstan."

"I have never mentioned that case. That was on the Illogan side of the district and was not on my side."

Captain Thomas switched track. "There was the case of Ivey, at Tuckingmill. Do you call that typhoid fever? The man was only in a bed a few days and had nothing more than a feverish cold. There was also the case of Bennetts, who was only away thirteen days. Was that typhoid fever?"

"I call that a case of a very mild type."

"But the man was only in bed six days, and the highest medical authorities will tell you that this could not be typhoid fever. I could give many such cases."

"Will you please do so," responded Mr. Angove, and waited.

"There was the case of the man Cadwell, who was only in bed a very few days. You said Bennett's case was typhoid fever, whereas it was nothing but a cold. The idea of a man being home six days with typhoid fever!"

Captain Thomas's face was reddening. Mr. Angove, the qualified medical expert, remained calm.

"It is quite possible. A man might have a mild form of typhoid, without having the ulceration of the bowels, which *attends the more serious cases, and in a case of that kind he might quickly get better."*

"But you reported a case some time since of typhoid fever, of a man who was only away from the mine six days."

"I said it was a case of a typhoid type." Mr. Angove's patience had reached its limit. "All I can say is that if men are driven to work in that way it is no wonder that so much decline prevails among them. These poor men are driven to work when they are not fit to go, and they frequently die of miner's decline."

Everyone at that meeting knew what he meant when Mr. Angove referred to miner's decline. It was the white plague; other names such as consumption, scrofula, hectic fever, or graveyard cough all helped identify the effects. Or simply phthisis. Going down a mine brought lung disease and, for many, death.

"I don't know what you mean by being driven. We never drive them!"

Captain Thomas was by now an angry man. But other people were up in arms, too.

Quick as a flash, the worthy and progressive Mr. Pike retorted, "No. Necessity drives them!"

Captain Thomas was not to be out done. "But you know, Mr. Pike, that they are not cases of typhoid fever."

"No. I do not know it," responded Mr. Pike, with laughter from others now breaking the tension in the room.

Captain Thomas was like a limpet. Back he came. "There could not have been more than two or three cases, so far as our men are concerned."

Mr. Angove saw the gap in the man's defences. "How can that be, when four of them died?"

Captain Thomas may have been skewered, but he was

not finished. "All I can say is this, that the water is now being brought into the mine from the Camborne Waterworks, and today the men actually appealed to me not to have any more of it. They preferred the other."

Perhaps some of the men were reluctant to forsake the old taste, but that was not the point here. These men were becoming ill, and many were dying, because of their foul working conditions. As Mr. Angove indicated in his report, in the last two years there had been eighty-two deaths from phthisis. Mining was killing miners.

It took time for the elephant in the room to be fully revealed. As we have noted (see above, p.33), it was the 1842 Royal Commission that first showed the extent of lung disease amongst Cornish miners and their report had led directly to an investigation into adult Cornish miners' ill health by Dr. William Farr, of the Registrar General's Office. The Victorian state was beginning to grapple with the consequences of an unregulated capitalism that was in full flow at a time when medical understanding of the human body's responses to working conditions was still a work in progress.

Farr proved through his use of statistics that Cornish miners had an excess mortality that was peculiar to class and mainly attributable to respiratory organ disease, commonly known as miners' phthisis. His results were published in the 1864 Royal Commission Report into the Condition of Mines, which repeated the 1842 assertion that poor air, due to imperfect ventilation, was to blame. The scientific and medical understanding of the causation of silicosis had not yet been grasped. However, the 1864 report did acknowledge accessory causes for the excess mortality, such as ladder-climbing, sudden temperature changes, and the inhalation of gritty particles. The recommendations made included the inspection of mines and increasing ventilation to the mines' ends, and these were made law in the Metalliferous Mines Act of 1872.

By the 1870s, inadequate ventilation seemed established as the explanation for the high incidence of lung disease among Cornish miners. However, when Robert Koch, the German physician and microbiologist, discovered the tubercle bacillus in 1882, a new consensus emerged that all cases of phthisis were tuberculosis infections. The understanding of silicosis was still not yet developed.

It was within this context of a partial scientific and medical understanding that a new outbreak of illness occurred among Cornish miners at the turn of the century. The second source above highlights a couple of the findings of the Royal Commission into the Health of Cornish Tin Miners that had been set up in 1904 to investigate this outbreak. It was led by John Scott Haldane, the Scottish physician and physiologist, who had developed a national reputation for expertise in the causes of miners' ill health, and it discovered that most of the current disease was due to an infection by the ankylostoma hookworm that had been brought to Cornish mines by men who had worked in the tropics.

As we have already seen, explaining what happened in Cornish mines needs a global perspective. The onset of the Boer War (1899-1902) in South Africa led to men who had emigrated returning to Cornwall. The hookworm infestation that came back with them further weakened already vulnerable bodies, leading to increased morbidity. This hookworm could only survive in hot mines; the symptoms of the disease were anaemia and rashes. Transmission was faecal-oral, and the epidemic was evidently due to a lack of sanitation in the mines. The Royal Commission identified the cause – and then blamed the miners. Their dirty habits, defecating in the mines, had caused the outbreak. Working class ignorance was to blame. The lack of provision of adequate sanitation by the mine owners was not formally addressed.

At the Bassets' Dolcoath mine, where there were the most cases of ankylostomiasis, measures were taken to clear up the excrement, which was assumed to cause the rashes by direct contact with the skin. These included, on the advice of local doctors, a fan being placed at the top of the mine shaft to cure the anaemia. Better ventilation was always good, but it was no cure for anaemia. Nevertheless, one way or another, the worm had almost been eradicated by the time Haldane arrived and he only needed to advise a few further preventive measures, such as quarantine, to end the infection. But it was Haldane, despite his medical and scientific experience and knowledge, who could not bring himself to place the responsibility for the outbreak with the employers who had failed to meet the sanitary needs of their workers by providing adequate toilet facilities.

I quoted Friedrich Engels in an earlier section (p.17-18), describing the sanitary horrors of Manchester in 1844. In my doctoral thesis, I also referenced the view of the historian Stephen Marcus (New York, 1974) that it was around this mid-century period that some within the middle class – and he takes Engels as a radical example – began to be conscious that 'millions of English men, women, and children were virtually living in shit.' However, it seems that many in the middle classes remained blind. They shied away from the question why such unhealthy closeness to human excrement might still be commonplace, a half century later.

***

The work of A.K. Hamilton Jenkin, *Cornish Miner* (1927/72), is a rich source of material for exploring the interface between working class miners and those in the middle classes. His research throws further light on the reasons for ill health and death in the mining community. He notes that those who published papers in the Royal Cornwall Polytechnic Society in the 1840s and 1850s were among the first to draw attention to the dangers of mining life. In 1835, the manager of the United Mines in Cornwall could assert that copper mines were well-ventilated and that 'tin mines are perhaps the healthiest of all.' But by 1847, the alternative view was spelt out in one such Polytechnic paper:

> 'Think of the fact that nearly one out of every five Gwennap miners incurs a violent death to produce the staple commodity which most contributes to the wealth of this county… [Gwennap was a largely copper mining area, north-west of Camborne, that had been known as the 'richest square mile in the old world' in the late eighteenth and early nineteenth centuries]… About one in every million railway travellers has been stated to be killed by railway accidents and the country rings with demands for inquiry and prevention… while of the miners working in a single parish of this county, nineteen in every hundred die a violent death, and it has only

been by your Society that attention has been called to
the subject or active measures encouraged to remedy
the evil.'

Between 1857 and 1859, Dr. Richard Couch, a mine surgeon
in West Cornwall, investigated the working lifespan of a
Cornish miner. He concluded that:

'The active life of a miner supposing it to commence
at ten years of age, terminates in eighteen years, at the
very early age of twenty-eight, when, in most other
occupations, he would be in the prime of manhood
and vigour.'

Dr. Couch estimated that the average death-age was forty-
seven, giving a period of nineteen years of unproductive life,
during which the miner was either unable to work, due to
accident or disease, or driven to seek lighter work on the
surface. James Mager's death as a surface worker in 1889 (see
above, pp.28-33) fits neatly into this time scale.

How much did Cornish miners earn for selling their
labour? A little touch of Karl Marx's ideas helps to provide
a context for exploring this question of earnings. Marx saw
labour-power as a commodity. The labourer is a free agent
who owns his own person and comes to the marketplace as
the legal equal of the owner of money. The labourer freely
sells his labour, he puts it at the disposal of the buyer, and
in so doing alienates himself from his labour. He cannot sell
the commodities his labour has produced; the labourer does
not own the means of production and therefore cannot fully
enjoy the fruits of his labour. A tin miner is compelled to

obtain the money to feed and clothe and shelter himself and family by selling his labour-power to someone else, who can then sell the refined tin on the open market.

The research of Hamilton Jenkin throws a remarkable light on the degree of exploitation suffered by the Cornish miner in this legal transaction with the owner of money. For instance, until 1872, when the miner became entitled to be paid every month, for four weeks work, the old Cornish system of reckoning by the calendar or 'five-week month' was maintained, which meant that every three months the miner had to work an extra week. Moreover, the two categories that determined how miners were to be paid for selling their labour-power were established by the owners of money and worked, overall, to their advantage and against the miners.

Cornish miners were paid either by tutwork (in a fixed contract which specified the wage) or tribute (in an arrangement that gave the miner a share in the value of the ore he had mined). Work associated with the development of the mine, such as the shaft-sinking and cross-cutting necessary for reaching the tin-bearing lodes, was done by tut workers. Tributers, however, were employed on the lode only and were paid a certain percentage of every pound's worth they sent to the surface. Hamilton Jenkin remarks:

'Both tutwork and tribute were to a certain extent a gamble; the former depending on the nature of the country rock and the latter on the quality of the mineral vein or lode. "You set a pair of men and give them £4 a fathom," said a captain in 1864, speaking of tutwork, "and before they have driven six feet the ground will become such that they ought to have £7 or £8 to make a living".[16]

Despite the nearly equal risks and hardships, the tributer held a higher status within the mining community than the tut worker; his wage was, on average, higher. Hamilton Jenkin provides an example of a tributers' 'bal bill' (a mine pay-bill) for August 1863, the earnings – and the deductions! - for a group of six miners from Cook's Kitchen Mine in the Camborne region:

Cook's Kitchen Mine. (6)									
Pay for August, 1863.									
Paid 19th September, 1863.									
———— and Partners (6 men).									
Amount earned at 11s. 6d. in £ = £51 9 9									
Deductions.									
				£	s.	d.	£	s.	d.
Candles per lb.	...	...	...	2	15	6			
Powder ditto	...	...	...	1	3	4			
Fuse ⎫									
Hilts ⎪									
Shovels ⎬	...	...	...	...	0	11	2		
Cans ⎪									
Clay ⎭									
Smith Cost	...	...	...	...	1	0	5		
Drawing	...	...	...	...	2	12	9		
Weighing, Mixing, and Dividing	...	—							
Tramming	...	...	...	...	—				
Sample	...	...	...	...	0	9	0		
Subsist	...	...	...	...	16	14	0		
Doctor and Club	...	...	...	0	8	0			
Barber and Box	...	...	...	0	4	0			
							25	18	2
Debt	...	...	...				1	18	0
							£23	13	7

These six miners had agreed a tribute arrangement whereby they received 57.5 per cent (11s 6d in £) of the value of the tin ore they had mined, leaving them with a month's earnings of £51 9s 9d.[17]

However, the mine owners then deducted a substantial

16   £4 in 1864 = c.£564 today; £7 = c.£987 today; £8 = c.£1,128
17   £51 9s 9d in 1863 = c.£6,827 today

number of costs, a practice that trade unions came to regard as flagrant exploitation. This company of six miners had to pay not only for their own candles, powder, fuses, barrels, nails, pick-hilts, shovels, and other materials necessary for breaking the ore, but also for the tramming of it to the shaft, the drawing to surface, and the subsequent crushing, weighing, mixing, dividing, and sampling of the ores. In addition, there was the large deduction (£16 14s) – around two-thirds of the total deduction (£23 13s 7d) – for subsistence, the repayment of an advance of ready money paid to them by the mining company in a previous month when the miners had not earned enough to meet their basic needs. The mine owners needed to ensure their young, skilled workforce was retained. Finally, there were the deductions for the weekly shave provided by the mine barber (4s), and the cost of the mine doctor and the mines' club (8s) – there is more on the mines' clubs below. All these deductions meant the six miners were left with £23 13s 7d, around half of the nominal value of their month's work.[18] It may still have been a sum that made miners richer than farmers or fishermen, but there was no regularity or certainty of income, and ill health and an early death awaited.

Hamilton Jenkin provides the detail that shows how the mine owners controlled not only the wages that were paid to the miner in work but also the medical support the miner needed in sickness. The health of the miner was yet again subject to the decisions of the wealthy and powerful through the so-called 'mine club' into which the miners paid a monthly subscription varying between 6d and a shilling throughout

18   £23 13s 7d in 1863 = c.£3,427 today

their working lives. But such funds were effectively in the hands of the mine owners and managers, and the benefits varied very much from mine to mine. In most mines, the club granted only what was known as 'hurt pay', that is, relief at the rate of 1s a day for 'external and visible hurts.' Most mine managers knew the funds available were insufficient to cope with the demands from old men who were too weak to work underground any longer.

The large mines of the Camborne-Redruth district were, however, an exception. Captain W. Rutter, the manager of East Crofty, explained to the Royal Commissioners in 1864 that:

"The rule says it must be visible hurt, but we have always slipped it over as a matter of philanthropy, and we have relieved men when they have been home with severe colds, and so on... If a man has a broken leg, for example, we pay for persons watching him and bandages, and anything he wants. If he wants a bed or mattress, or anything of that sort, we have always given it. We have many men home for years who have been fairly worn out in the mine, because miners do not live to be very old."

The mine management was claiming the credit for providing welfare for sick miners from a fund which was created by those same miners. In addition to the deduction for the club (6d to 1s a month), a further subscription of 6d or 9d a month was taken from the miner's wages for the mine surgeon or doctor, who attended the men, and sometimes their families, in cases of sickness or accident. The mine doctor was appointed either by the adventurers, those speculators who were investing their funds into the mining enterprise, or the mineral lords who also had their ownership claims on the mines.

Captain Rutter further explained that at East Crofty, when the club fund became exhausted, an appeal would be made to the men to pay 2d in £1 more for a little while, 'and they do it with great pleasure.' In effect, this 'voluntary' extra payment would have meant that for every £1 (20 shillings) they earned by their labour, the miners received 19s 10d. Hamilton Jenkin adds the detail that the purser of Carn Brea mines, who was responsible for keeping the accounts, stated to the 1864 Commissioners that any man working in the mine 'has his coffin from the mine, and that is always charged to the club at Carn Brea.' He then comments that this was not the purser's kindness, but merely his common honesty in dealing with money which was not his own but the men's. Hamilton Jenkin concludes his section on this insurance scheme to help miners in poor health: '...the management of club money was, on the whole, perhaps one of the greatest scandals of the old regime.'

Further evidence of the corruption within this mining world comes from a witness, George Smith, Esq, who stated to the 1864 Commission that:

"I have often observed that when mines have been abandoned the men who have been permanently injured there have no means of getting their club money, notwithstanding that the mines may have produced a large sum of money which has been placed in these clubs. It has been taken by the purser or the

*secretary or otherwise been disposed of... I have seen
£300 or £400 – the balance of the money in the club –
appropriated to pay merchant's bills... I know of a case
in which a mine has stopped when the club money and
the doctor's money have been thrown back among the
parties to pay for a dinner that was given as the closing
of the affair."*[19]

As the source above (p.52) shows, Captain Rutter, the manager at East Crofty, knew that miners' club money had been used to reopen the East Crofty mine after the owners and adventurers had closed it down, leaving the miners without work and their access to their own funds gone. Rutter's reaction to this use of club money was clear: "*I told the purser, then and there, tooth and nail, that they were taking the blood and bones of the men.*"

George Smith, whose witness statement is quoted above, was so moved after talking to the miners themselves about this issue that he wrote a letter to the Mines Commission, in which he pleaded for the men to be able to choose their own surgeons and doctors:

'*Although the men but seldom loudly complain, and
are not forward, for obvious reasons, to speak on the
subject, I am convinced that there is among them an
extensive and deep-seated dissatisfaction with the
manner of these appointments, and not unfrequently
with the professional men who are so appointed.*'

---

19 £300 or £400 in 1864 = c.£40,600 or c.£54,100 today

Most miners lacked the means to alter the balance of power that was tilted in favour of their employers, but not all. Interestingly, Mr. Alfred Chennals reported to the Commissioners in 1864 that:

> *The miners in St Just have recently taken upon themselves to conduct the clubs. They have insisted, by a sort of rise in one or two cases, upon having control of their own moneys, and that the agents should no longer govern them, nor the adventurers in that respect.*

Such a move was exceptional. The miners were exchanging their labour, and their health, for the short-term gain of a wage – and they did so in an insecure world. The threat of mine closure and the loss of their income was always there. Migration was a possibility but the outcome an unknown. Moreover, those miners who worked as tributers were pitted one man, or one team, against another. So-called 'pitches' were determined within the mine and the men then bid against each other for the exclusive right to extract what they could from that pitch, receiving a set number of shillings for every pound's worth of ore they brought to the surface. In such circumstances of uncertainty, instances of Cornish miners acting together to further their own interests were generally fewer than for workers elsewhere in Britain.

Bernard Deacon (2007), formerly senior lecturer at the University of Exeter's Institute of Cornish Studies, has noted that Cornish miners were slow to join the new working class political institutions of the early nineteenth century – trade unions and Chartist groups. The Chartist missionaries who visited Cornwall in 1839 found the going tough, although Chartist branches were maintained during the 1840s in Penzance, Truro, Camborne, and St Ives. The first attempt to form a miners' union had to wait until 1866. Deacon also suggests that the teetotal movement in mid-nineteenth-century Cornwall, linked to the widespread influence of Methodism through its chapels, served to divert energies and enthusiasms away from political activity. My American friend and reader, Professor Doug Raber, suggests other factors too: religious belief and acceptance of Church authority would have played into the miner's acceptance of authority in general; the suspicion of outsiders such as union organisers; and the importance of endemic conservatism and resistance to change.

Nevertheless, the political momentum towards trade unionism and more democracy was gaining some ground, even in the world of Cornish mining. Progress, however, came in fits and starts. As Deacon (1986) has shown, Cornish miners took the opportunity of the 1872 economic boom to demand the end of the 'five-week month', the system of payment by calendar month that meant an occasional five-week gap between pay days. Among the first mineworkers to strike were the Wheal Basset bal maidens ('bal' being the Cornish for 'mine'). Bal maidens were female manual labourers working on the surface of the mines. From this epicentre at Illogan, the strike wave spread across the mining districts from Botallack in St Just to Okel Tor in Calstock. But some of the gains achieved through these strikes were lost with the fall in tin prices after 1873 and the consequent weakening of the miners' bargaining power. Strikes did, though, as Deacon notes, now become more frequent.

Remarkably, as the movement towards universal male suffrage gathered pace in the late-Victorian period, Camborne became, for a decade, a showpiece centre for political extremism. The thirty-two-year-old radical Charles Conybeare, the Miners' Friend (see above, pp.42-44), was able to win, albeit narrowly, the new Camborne-Redruth parliamentary seat in 1885, to be re-elected in 1896, and hold the seat until 1895. Conybeare had few family connections in Cornwall, but he offered one of the most progressive platforms in the UK. He was anti-landlord. He called for the abolition of the House of Lords, the disestablishment of the Church of England, a graduated income tax, Sunday closing of pubs, votes for women, triennial elections, and Home Rule. The miners knew they had Conybeare on their side. 'For a moment, the mining constituency shone out as a beacon of the new democratic politics, occupying a place at the leading edge of British politics' (Deacon, 1992/2007).

Conybeare proposed changes to the Stannaries Act of 1855 to end the system whereby miners still sometimes had their pay shared out in a public house. Stannery law, dating back to the early fourteenth century, is a body of English law that governed tin mining in Devon and Cornwall. It still formally exists but was effectively ended by the Stannaries Court (Abolition) Act of 1896. He also sought protection from mine agents who randomly broke contracts of employment, and he advocated a mines inspector drawn from working miners, with the aim of reducing the high mortality in Cornish mines. However, his anti-establishment views and actions brought trouble in its wake. In 1889, he was imprisoned in Derry Gaol for helping to distribute bread to destitute, evicted Irish tenants.

The place for Camborne-Redruth at the cutting edge of British radicalism had only been temporary. The further development of low-cost tin reserves in Bolivia and Malaya was adding to the economic pressures on mining in Cornwall. As Deacon (2007) concludes: 'The miners who made up the backbone of Conybeare's voters began to disperse again to seek work overseas.'

Working class solidarity, in so far as it could be achieved in the context of Cornish mining, was not able to be sustained given the disrupting influence of the migration of the miners themselves to other lands. It is no surprise that Conybeare lost his seat in 1895, nor that miners should continue to be blamed for their own insanitary conditions and ill health.

THE POOR MAN AT HIS GATE – THE DANGERS OF LIFE AT THE MINE: INJURY AND DEATH BY FIRE, WATER, AND EARTH

Sources:
The Newry Telegraph – Saturday 27 June 1868:

Terrible Gunpowder Explosion

On Saturday morning a series of explosions of gunpowder and gun-cotton took place at Dolcoath mine, near Camborne… It is too apparent that sufficient care was not manifested in the withdrawing of [the miners' gunpowder] to prevent some loose powder and cotton from falling outside the cupboards. Three brothers, James Oliver Walter, 9; Augustus Walter, 7; and Alfred Lewis Walter, 5 years of age, started from their home to accompany their sister to Pengegon, where she was going to fetch water. They were joined by a little boy named Thomas Keel, 7, and in passing through Dolcoath mine on the way to the well, the four lads turned aside into the magazine court, "to look for powder". Having collected together all the loose grains that were about, they ignited some matches, with which they had previously provided themselves, and set fire to the powder. The flames communicated to one of the bottom cupboards and instantly there were several explosions... The poor lads, who were frightfully burnt, were at once attended to, but three of them died the same evening, and the fourth the following day.

Morpeth Herald – Saturday 18 February 1888:

Mr. James Bolitho, of Bolenowe, Camborne, was engaged on Monday at the South Condurrow Mine, near Camborne, in blasting a hole, when the explosive ignited prematurely, inflicting terrible injuries on Mr. Bolitho, whose recovery is hopeless.

Cornish & Devon Post – Saturday 14 January 1893:

MINE FLOODED AT ST. JUST. SEVERAL LIVES LOST. HEROIC DEEDS

Wheal Owles' tin mine, near St. Just, was on Tuesday morning the scene of a terrible disaster.... An unknown working filled with water may lurk in almost any ground where mining has been carried on in years gone by, and to cut into one of these means the flooding of the mine.... They [The twenty-one miners of the forty-one 'who only an hour or two before had gone to their work in good spirits'] got to the surface, and a most excited state it was. Their first words were, however, of sympathy for their poor comrades whose bodies they had left below, and their next of profound thankfulness for their own escape... About nine o'clock they heard a tremendous report, which one man described as like ten thousand thunders. The shock appalled them, and at first those working in other parts of the mine were dumbfounded. In a moment or two, however, they heard the swish of water, and then everywhere there was the cry, "The water has broken away." Then followed a mad scramble for life up the narrow ladder way, which was the only escape. With the inrush of water came the rapid rush of air, and some of the men were literally forced up the shaft. There were some heroic scenes too... Only at the mouth of the shaft were the miners able to see how many of their comrades had been drowned, and it was found that twenty had perished.... Of the cause of the accident, it is of course, only possible to conjecture.

Manchester Daily Examiner & Times – Thursday 21 September 1893:

DREADFUL SITUATION – EIGHT MEN MISSING

A Camborne correspondent telegraphs that a dreadful accident occurred yesterday at the well-known Dolcoath Mine, Cornwall. Two levels collapsed and 30 miners were entombed. Some men who were injured were brought to the surface and others, afterward. Eight men, however, are still entombed. It is feared that there is very little chance of reaching them through the heavy falls of stuff until – supposing they are not injured they are in a state of starvation. Six of them are married, and four of them have families.

The lode in which the debris fell is about 30 ft wide, and the timberman, with a staff of men, was securing the ground there when it fell on them with scarcely any warning....

The accident is the most serious which has occurred in a Cornish mine since the flooding of the Wheal Owles last January, when 20 men lost their lives. The Dolcoath Mine is the largest and richest tin mine in the world, and the spot where the accident occurred is where the richest deposit of tin ore is found....

The rush of air following the fall of earth was very powerful, many of the survivors being thrown down with violence, and a heavy wagon was hurled many yards away and survived overturned. The work of the mine is not likely to be greatly interfered with.

Bad news, they say, travels fast – and reports that feature multiple deaths in sensational circumstances have always been grist in the media mill. As the sources above show, news of Cornish mining tragedies was taken up and presented in detail in far-flung parts of the nation: Newry in Ireland, Morpeth in Northumberland, Manchester in Lancashire. Mining for metallic ore or coal were activities of interest across the nation. It was a focus for all those people whose lives were directly shaped by the geological substructure of the land on which they lived. And since the natural deposits within the strata below the surface were helping fuel the industrial revolution, it was also a focus for all those who, wherever they lived, had a financial interest in making money from the extraction of these profitable ores and carbons.

The '*terrible gunpowder explosion*' in the summer of 1868 was even more dreadful and sensational because children had been killed. The account in *The Newry Telegraph* in 1868 provides the detail that offers insights into both how young children in a mining community spent their time on a Saturday morning, and the absence of adequate health and safety measures within the territory of the mine:

> '*The miners are accustomed to receive their supplies of powder and gun-cotton, for blasting, every Monday morning, and the quantity thus received, amounting from 10lb to 50lb, for each "pair" of men, is stored in a number of small cupboards arranged against the wall of an open court, situate near the copper floors. Each cupboard is supplied with a lock, the key of which is in the possession of the pair of men whose powder is stored in it, and who are accustomed to take from it only as much as will suffice for the day's requirements.*'

Then comes the evidence for how the blame-game was played out in such industrial accidents. The responsibility for the explosion that killed four children lay with the miners, not the mining company, according to this media report which asserts: '*It is too apparent that sufficient care was not manifested in the withdrawing of this supply to prevent some loose powder from falling outside the cupboards.*'

The three young brothers from the Walter family set out from home around 10 am, following their thirteen-year-old sister, who had been delegated the task of fetching water from Pengegon, the upmarket end of Camborne as noted above (p.38). It was an important responsibility, obtaining drinkable water from an uncontaminated well. The seven-year-old boy, Thomas Keel, joined the expedition and as the source above reported, all four boys died within twenty-four hours from their burns after the explosion that followed their 'powder play.' They had slipped away from the unnamed sister to have their fun with matches and powder. The newspaper account explains that their sister rushed in whilst the lockers were exploding, presumably alerted to the disaster by the sound of the blasts, and: '*snatching up [one of her injured brothers] carried him to a place of safety, herself escaping without a burn.*'

The failures of the mining company in this industrial accident show a remarkable disregard for the value of human life. Whatever the casual acceptance by the miners of the dangers they faced, it is disturbing to find that those who employed them were so negligent in the storage and supervision of explosives. Such disregard for health and safety had been endemic throughout the history of the copper and tin industry, and other industries, too, which depended on the labour of the working class. In part, there is a crude calculation at play here: health and safety measures would cost money and such an outlay would reduce profits for the owners and shareholders. Yet something is apparent here which is more complex and nastier, with its roots, I suggest, in fear. The industrial revolution needed its workers; the working class was created because of industrialisation and urbanisation. But there were so many more workers than owners of capital. What if the workers were to revolt? The memories of the French revolution at the end of the eighteenth century and the social upheavals that followed were entrenched in the minds of those privileged by the possession of wealth and power. Workers were needed, no doubt, but they had to be controlled. They could be dangerous. A fear of the many who were so different from the privileged few would have been largely unacknowledged in a pre-Freudian world. But such a fear does help explain the disregard and contempt for the lives and welfare of most of the population.

The times were beginning to change, however. I have already argued that a new way of looking at the world was becoming apparent (see above, pp.15-17). An alternative structure of feeling was emerging, one that was more humane. Yet it seems likely that the imminent death of James Bolitho in 1888, following the '*terrible injuries*' he sustained when '*explosives used for blasting ignited prematurely*' (see the second source above), would have been shrugged off by the mine managers and owners as unfortunate collateral in a mining enterprise that was self-justificatory. Captain James Rowe had already made the argument 'firmly', in the public meeting in August 1864 (see above, p.15): "*...since most of the inhabitants earn their living by mining, the rate of mortality must necessarily be high.*"

Rest in peace, James Bolitho and the four children, James Oliver Walter, Augustus Walter, Alfred Lewis Walter, and Thomas Keel.

***

The *Cornish & Devon Post* (see the third source above) provided details of the occasion on Tuesday 10 January 1893 when twenty miners lost their lives in the space of a few minutes, working underground within the Wheal Owles mine at St Just, around twenty-three miles south-west of Camborne. This tragedy was taken as further unfortunate collateral in the mining enterprise. Their demise was accidental. However, contemporary newspaper reports yield detail that suggests an alternative verdict – and, as we will see, a government prosecution succeeded in delivering a minor tap on the knuckles.

The Western Morning News is credited by the *Cornish & Devon Post* as giving *'a graphic description of the disaster'* and is then quoted:

> 'It is a very old mine, and now includes in its "sett" the ground which was formerly worked by other mining companies… All round it, therefore, almost, indeed, for miles around, the land is literally honeycombed with levels and old workings, which have naturally become the repository for tons and tons of water which have percolated from the surface, or fallen down the many shafts and inlets, so that without an adequate knowledge of the exact whereabouts of each of the old workings, mining must… be attended with some amount of danger. [Cutting into an unknown working filled with water] is exactly what must have happened at Wheal Owles.'

So much was beyond dispute. The description continues, referencing the ownership and management of the mine. It seems the once prosperous mine had only small lodes of tin remaining, and the shareholders had been warned that the property could not last long. The majority shareholders were 'Messrs. Bolitho and Sons [of Cornwall] and Messrs. Weston and Bellingham, of London.' The manager of the mine was Mr. Richard Boyne, but since he was in ill health most of the business had been conducted for some time by his son, Mr. Herbert Boyne. The underground management of the mine was undertaken by Captains Tom Tregear and John Leggo, *'two persons of excellent reputation as miners.'*

Neither of these two captains were underground at the time of the disaster. Captain Tregear saw some of the miners scrambling up the ladder ways in great haste and learned from these '*terribly alarmed*' men that the water had broken in underground. Tregear descended to the level of the adit, the safety valve of the mine since the water could not rise above it, where an almost exhausted and breathless man named Hall – the last man to leave the mine alive - passed by him, heading for the surface. Tregear descended further to the thirty fathoms level, where he reached the water level. '*He peered into the water with the hope of seeing something of those who had been left below, but his search was in vain, and finding he could go no further, he beat a retreat.*'

Back on the surface, news of the disaster soon spread in the district and messengers quickly found the homes of those who had met their fate. The official figures show that there were seven women widowed that morning and twenty-three children orphaned. Work in the district was '*almost entirely suspended.*'

This newspaper source relayed some of what it called the '*pathetic incidents told of the poor fellows who were drowned*', and in so doing provides invaluable information about the influence of evangelical Christianity in the lives of some of these twenty victims. Five of the twenty victims had an acknowledged active Christian life. Three of them had worshipped together the night before they died. They were Thomas Grose, who was single and perished with his widower father, John Grose; William Eddy who was single; and William Thomas Davey, also single, who had only recently returned from the North of England and gone underground for the first time the previous Tuesday. They were all present on the previous evening at the annual meeting of the Band of Hope (a Temperance movement linked to the Methodist Wesleyan Society) '*and were in the best of spirits.*' Thomas Grose had been the assistant secretary, resigning his position at that meeting; '*a young man very well liked and highly spoken of.*' Thomas Ellis was another victim with a Methodist life; he had been the organist at the Bible Christian Chapel and married with two children. Edward White, who also drowned, was the superintendent of the Sunday School at Dowran and married with one child.

As for the cause of the tragedy, which is already in the newspaper report categorised as an '*accident*', that was left open to conjecture. The reports of men who were near at the time indicated that the water broke through at the end of the sixty-five fathom level, which had been driven in about fifty fathoms from the shaft.[20] John Taylor, married with two children, was working there, '*and it is supposed – though it is mere supposition – that he tapped the water whilst working in the end.*' The inrush of water was '*tremendous*', coming it seems from three mines: Wheal Drea, the unworked part of Wheal Owles, and east Boscean. The report continued:

> '*If the presumed cause of the accident is the correct one, it must have been an old working which is not shown on the existing plans... The greatest care had always been taken – because the danger has always been so apparent – to have careful drillings so that the old workings might be avoided, and this it was thought had been done... Captain Tom Tregear said he was*

---

20   65 fathom level = 390 feet – calculate 6 feet to a fathom from here on

unable to explain how the accident occurred, because the agents had not the slightest idea that they were near water.'

The media account of the tragedy as an *'accident'* is likely to have chimed with the reaction of the owners, shareholders, and managers to one of the worst disasters in Cornish mining history. First, however, there was the immediate concern: how to help all those in the mining community affected by what had happened at the Wheal Owles mine. Such suffering required a tangible Christian response, and the Methodist ministers were on the scene shortly before the Anglican vicar:

'Amongst those who were early at the mine were the [two] Wesleyan ministers – and they were shortly followed by the [Anglican] vicar, Rev. J. Andrews Reeve, who, after conferring with the agents, proceeded to visit the widows and friends of the deceased men, and to relieve any immediate necessities. The representative of Messrs. Borlass, one of the lords [with a title of ownership for the mine], was also on the spot making inquiries…'

The local establishment would have been shaken by this tragedy. Mining as an enterprise might lead to early deaths – but rarely on this scale.

Just over a fortnight after the disaster, the *Royal Cornwall Gazette* carried this headline on Thursday 26 January 1893: *'THE RELIEF FUND – SHOULD THE SURPLUS GO FROM ST. JUST?'*

It is illuminating to follow the discussion in the St Just

meeting of the Wheal Owles relief fund committee meeting on the previous Monday, with the local vicar, Rev. J. Andrews Reeve, in the chair. Matters became controversial when the issue of an over-subscription to the fund was raised and, with it, the question of where that surplus might go within the county. Dr. Searle insisted that any surplus ought to be banked exclusively for St Just. Any suggestion that moneys should be taken from a poor district like St Just into a rich district like Camborne and Redruth was unacceptable.

Such matters, however, remained hypothetical. So far, £2,144 had been promised to the relief fund – comprising £1,125 from the Mine and the adventurers, and £1,019 from general subscriptions – and of this sum, £1,353 had been paid into the bank. It was formally agreed that they would require £3,500 'to put the relatives in a fairly good position.'[21] The vicar, from the chair, remarked:

> *We must do this work generously and fairly. We need to give the poor things what we can now. I have had applications from several orphanages for some of the children, especially from Dr. Barnardo, whose secretary is coming to Penzance in a few weeks and would be glad to take a child back with him."*

To a twenty-first-century ear, such deliberations may seem a long way removed from the immediate needs of those affected by the disaster. There were, nevertheless, decisions taken at this meeting about charity grants to survivors that did provide

---

21   £2,144 in 1893 = c.£306,590 today; £1,125 = c.£160,870 today; £1,019 = c.£145,720 today; £1,353 = c.£193,480 today; £3,500 = c.£500,000 today

relief. Those underground miners who had survived and now found themselves '*thrown out of employment*' by the closure of the mine (twenty-one men) would get grants of £2 10s each, '*equal to about a fortnight's pay... it being understood that they would have no further claim on the fund.*' Each of the widows would get a temporary grant of 10s a week, with the other dependent relatives receiving 5s a week, this being subject to revision when a permanent scheme had been formulated.

In effect, such arrangements meant that the twenty-one surviving miners would take a once and for all sum of £52 10s from the fund. The seven widows and twenty-three dependent children would draw £9 5s a week, a yearly sum of £481. If the relief fund were to reach £3,500, it would have taken around seven years to exhaust its funds.[22]

Death by Water - the victims of the Wheal Owles mine disaster are recorded on this memorial plaque, close to the surface remains of the mine. Weathering has begun to make it difficult to instantly read the script. Here are the names of the victims:

Thomas Allen, Lewis Blewett Wilkins, Peter Dale, William Davey, William Eddy, James Edwards Trembath, Thomas Ellis, John Grose, Thomas Grose, Charles Hichens Thomas, John Olds (Bosanko), William Roberts, James Rowe, William Stevens Thomas, John Taylor, Mark Taylor, James Thomas, Edward White, Edward Williams, James Williams.

22 £2 10s in 1893 = c.£357.50 today; 10s = c.£71.50; £52 10s = c.£7,508; £9 5s = c.£1,323; £481 = c.£69,000; £3,500 = c.£500,000

Those who had wealth and power in the local community understood that this was an occasion when an attachment to the values of the Christian religion had to be visibly demonstrated. They also had an understanding that the issue of responsibility for the disaster would, in time, be settled by legal judgement. On Thursday 13 April 1893, the *Cornish Telegraph* carried a report that a Treasury prosecution was being heard at the West Penwith petty sessions before two West Penwith magistrates, the Rev. J. Tonkin and Mr. C.C. Ross. The long arm of late-Victorian criminal justice was extending from London to the Penwith peninsula of Cornwall. Mr. A.E. Archer prosecuted on behalf of the Treasury and Mr. G.I. Bodilly defended. Mr. Richard Boyne, the manager who had been so incapacitated by ill health that his son, Herbert Boyne, had been doing most of the business for some time, was accused of failing '*to keep in the office at the mine an accurate plan of the workings of the mine, showing the workings up to at least six months previously*', as required by the Metalliferous Mines Regulation Act of 1872.

Mr. Bodilly addressed the Court for the defence:

"Purser Boyne has been manager of the mine for more than 40 years. His pride has always been in showing that the mine was in a right and proper order for working. As far as his knowledge has allowed him, he has kept the plans of the mine in a complete and efficient way. Indeed, Mr. Boyne kept a plan twenty years before he was compelled to do so by the legislation of 1872.

"Unfortunately for the defendant, and more unfortunately still for the poor fellows who lost their lives in this sad accident, he did not know, never had

known, and never had appreciated, the fact that the variations in the magnetic north would have any appreciable effect on the bearings of the mine.

"You have all here in Court been most surprised to find that the variations in the compass since 1841 have caused a difference of 46 fathoms in the mine from shaft to shaft. Observing and acting upon these variations would require some degree of scientific skill. You have heard Mr. Archer for the prosecution argue that a person who did not know that the magnetic north varied had no business to keep a mine plan, but I put it to you that this criminal charge against Purser Boyne fails to take account of the requirements of section 19 of the 1872 Act…"

I asked an acquaintance of mine, a mining expert, about the significance of shifts in magnetic north in this instance. He was dismissive, pointing out that in a mine, in any case, there was so much material made from iron that would affect a magnetic compass reading. The matter of magnetic north variations was irrelevant. I learned enough to suspect that the defence lawyer was attempting to blind the Court through the assertion of scientific facts that, even if true, were of no consequence to the case. The two magistrates hearing the case seem to have come to the same conclusion. On Saturday 22 April 1893, the *Derbyshire Courier* carried this headline: '*A MINE CAPTAIN FINED*' and reported that last Saturday the magistrates had imposed a fine of £15 and costs upon Captain Boyne, manager of Wheal Owles Mine.[23]

---

23   £15 in 1893 = c.£2,150 today

And so, a rap on the knuckles had been delivered. A measure of justice obtained, albeit a very small one. Today, we would call this disaster criminal negligence of the first order, a case of corporate manslaughter.

The memorial plaque and location of the Cargodna shaft at Wheal Owles. (Source: Julian Hodgson, through Flickr, who took these images in 2017 and has kindly granted permission for their use)[24]

Rest in peace, all twenty victims of the Wheal Owles mine disaster.

***

The *Manchester Daily Examiner & Times* (see the fourth source above) carried this headline on Thursday 21 September 1893: '*DREADFUL SITUATION – EIGHT MEN MISSING*'. It went on to provide an account of the collapse the day before of two levels within the Dolcoath Mine, leading to the entombment of thirty miners. Twenty-two had been rescued but eight remained trapped with no hope of rescue. Their

---

24   Source: Julian Hodgson, through Flickr, who took these images in 2017 and has kindly granted permission for their use.

tragic death was anticipated. The newspaper report, with its detail that six of these eight miners were married and four of them had children, anticipates the consequences of such a disaster: charitable donations, it states, will be needed to provide aid to the six widows and the dependent children.

The Glasgow Herald gave the names of the eight miners in their report on Friday 22 September 1893:

'*James Adams, 33, Tuckingmill, wife*
'*Frederick John Harvey, 30, Camborne, wife*
'*Richard James, 34, Illogan Highway, wife and five children*
'*John Henry Jennings, 20, Camborne, single*
'*William John Osborne, 32, Camborne, single*
'*John Pollard, 25, Chief Timberman, Camborne, wife and three children*
'*Charles White, 58, Senior timberman, Camborne, wife only*
'*Richard Davies, 18, Troon, single – Buried, but rescued after 37 hours.*'

The Manchester Daily Examiner & Times report stated that the work to remove the debris was necessarily slow, as:

'*...the material has to be drawn to the surface at the rate of 10 tons an hour, for there is no room at the bottom of the mine, where the men are buried, to remove the stuff on one side.*'

The lode in which the debris fell had been about thirty feet wide. John Pollard, the chief timberman, with a staff of men,

'...was securing the ground there when it fell on them with scarcely any warning.' The rush of air that followed was so powerful that 'a heavy wagon was hurled many yards away and overturned.' The report finishes with a conclusion that would have brought relief to owners and shareholders alike: 'The work of the mine is not likely to be greatly interfered with.'

In this report of what was recognised as 'the most serious accident which has occurred in a Cornish mine since the flooding of the Wheal Owles last January', the disaster is already categorised as an 'accident'; any charge of corporate manslaughter rests a hundred years or so in the future. The inquest in October 1893 confirmed that this was indeed an accident.

After the inquest, the account in *The Western Morning News* (10 October 1893) indicated that the jury had heard Captain Josiah Thomas, the mine manager, state he had been in the very place where the accident occurred the previous day and 'considered the stull [a round timber used to support the sides or back of a mine] to be perfectly safe.'

They had heard Captain James Johns, the underground agent, explaining that both he and Pollard had noticed two days before the accident that one of the timber supports was bending, and that would indicate movement: "...something was very heavy somewhere. But I saw no other piece bending and did not see any danger whatever."

They had heard David Jones, a mining student who was working with Pollard, testify: "...he had heard it said that the stoping [here meaning the open space left after the extraction of the ore] was rather high and that the timber hardly strong enough for it."

And after hearing all the evidence, the jury brought in

a verdict of 'Accidental Death' without retiring and passed a vote of sympathy with the relatives of the deceased and the Agents of the mine.

As the report in *The Manchester Daily Examiner & Times* acknowledges, '...*the Dolcoath Mine was the largest and richest tin mine in the world*', and the spot where the accident happened was '*where the richest deposit of tin ore is found.*' The financial means to make mining safer were not lacking. What was missing was a humane valuing of the lives of the men who were making the owners and shareholders so rich.

The stulls at 412 level - an image taken by J.C. Burrows in 1893, the year of the roof collapse that killed seven men.[25]

Imagine the horror of what happened through the words of the rescued miner, Richard Davies. The man's full forename has been omitted from this account that appeared in the

25   Source: www.imagearchive.royalcornwallmuseum.org.uk

Sunderland Daily Echo and Shipping Gazette on Wednesday 27 September 1893, citing the *Camborne Daily News*. He is R. Davies. His full name is given in *The Glasgow Herald* report above; my Ancestry search led me to the 1891 England census, which revealed that the rescued miner was Richard Davies, then aged nineteen, a miner and single, living with his father, Joseph, aged forty-two, also a miner; his mother, Sarah, aged forty-one; his brother, Sidney, married and also aged nineteen, so probably his twin; his younger brother, George, aged seventeen and also a miner; and three other younger siblings. They lived in a terraced house in New Road in Troon; their neighbours were all mining families, nearly all Cornish, most born in Camborne.

Here is the twenty-one-year-old Richard Davies' account:

'*I was sawing a prop at the time of the disaster. I had not been sawing more than about three minutes when I heard some timber cracking, and then came a tremendous, deafening rush of stuff, which knocked me eight or nine feet away... at the bottom of the level. I was struck on the head and legs. My partners aimed to run, but they must have been knocked down where they stood and buried. When I came to myself a bit, I found I was face downwards, my head being lower than my heels, but I managed to turn on my left side. Then I felt round with my hands to learn what position I was in, but I could not move much, for across my body was a balk of timber. I found that the place was about five feet long, two feet wide, and three feet high; but the timber kept me down nearly flat. I remained in that position until Thursday midnight.*'

The disaster had happened the day before. Davies lay trapped for thirty-seven hours.

> 'The hope that the rescue party would come to my relief bore me up although a dread mounted that I might die of hunger or thirst. I shouted at the top of my voice for help, but no one could have heard me. I also called out to learn if any of my comrades were alive and near, but I found I was alone. I could tell from the smell after awhile that there was a dead body near. I cried for mercy a long time; I shall never forget it. I must have fallen asleep, for when on Thursday afternoon, about six, the relief party asked me whether I knew what day it was I replied it was Wednesday afternoon. When I knew they were so close I made a great effort, and after a long time I managed to turn in the small space, and I got in above the timber, a distance of about ten feet. I found it full of small hollow places. I got to where I could go no further, and then Smith, who lives near me at Troon, crawled in 30 feet on his belly. He said, "Are you near?" I replied, "I'm just touching." He came forward a bit further and said, "Give me your hand." Then he put out his hand and touched what he thought was mine; but it was something cold – it was a dead man's hand.'

Davies explained that when Smith had recovered from the shock, he got a hatchet passed in so that he, Davies, could widen the hole.

> 'I did this, and Smith backed out, for the hole was so small he could not turn. I crawled out after him. I felt

pretty well going out, but when I stood with the relief party I had to be supported.'

The name of the rescued miner, Davis (sic), appears again in *The Cornish Telegraph* on Thursday October 5, 1893, just over a fortnight after the Dolcoath mine disaster, in the report of the fortnightly meeting of the Camborne Local Board (see above, p.52-53), held in the church vestry room the previous Friday evening (29th September). At that meeting, the disaster at Dolcoath was the first item on the agenda. F.W. Thomas, aged thirty and a qualified financial clerk who was to rise to the rank of Secretary of a Public Company (Source: 1901 England Census), was in the chair; his father was Captain Josiah Thomas, the manager at Dolcoath Mine since the death of his father, Captain Charles Thomas Senior, in 1868 (see above, pp. 13-14). Captain Charles Thomas Junior, now aged sixty-two and a man we have already encountered in public meetings in 1864 and 1881, is also present, still an active, conservative voice. His death came in 1896. Other conservative voices present are the two Rowes, James the father and Josiah the son. It had been Captain James Rowe, now in 1893 aged seventy-eight, who had moved the vote of sympathy at the start of the meeting; Captains James Rowe and Charles Thomas (Junior) are the same conservative voices as heard in the 1864 public meeting (see above, pp.12-17); Josiah Rowe, aged thirty-six and a local accountant, is the son of Captain James Rowe. The voice of conservatism has been passed on to the next generation.

At the start of the meeting, the resolution proposed by Captain James Rowe was carried, expressing sympathy with the bereaved relatives of the victims of the recent disaster.

F.W. Thomas, that is Frederick Thomas, then spoke from the Chair: "*It has been an anxious time for myself, my father [Captain Josiah Thomas], and other officials at Dolcoath. My father and I were present at the mine for four days and four nights, apart from a brief period of three hours. Our relief and satisfaction were so great knowing that we had been able to rescue at least one man. I can honestly say, I would willingly go through a similar experience should circumstances unfortunately require it, if the same result were to be achieved.*"

Cries of "*Hear, hear*" resounded through the vestry room.

There is no tribute paid to miner Smith of Troon, who crawled on his belly the sixty feet, there and back, to make the rescue possible. '*When I took Davis (sic) to his parent's home on the Friday morning, I felt I was bringing the dead back to life.*'

Frederick Thomas may have cast himself as a miracle-worker, but what then happened to Richard Davies, the miner plucked from the jaws of death? Ancestry searches revealed no further trace of him. However, a footnote reference in a Wikipedia article about the Dolcoath Mine provided access to the booklet *The Great Dolcoath*, by Albert Bluett' (1898), in which Bluett described how he was taken as a guest deep into Dolcoath, to the very spot where Richard Davies had been trapped:

'*As I looked into the little cavity amongst rocks and timber from which the only man who escaped alive was taken, an involuntary shudder came over me at the thought of being doubled up in that hole, with darkness and death for companions, for a whole week (sic). "Where is he now?" I asked, remembering how frail he was when brought to the surface. "Oh," came the answer, "he went to America some time after, and is now working in South Africa".'*

Bravo, Richard Davies!

Back in the vestry room, Frederick Thomas continued: "*I know there has been a little doubt in some minds as to whether Osborne [one of the eight victims] was spoken to before he died. Well, there is now no doubt about the matter. Davis (sic) himself, after his rescue, told my father that he spoke to no one until the Thursday night. So, Captain Johns [the Dolcoath underground mine agent] must have had a conversation with Osborne. You gentlemen, members of this Board, knew Osborne perhaps better than any other of the victims. I think you will all agree that one thing might be truly said: Osborne has taught us how to live and has shown us how to die.*"

More cries of "*Hear, hear*" filled the vestry.

No media report of such a conversation between mine manager and the dying miner, Osborne, has surfaced. Did Captain Johns invent a conversation with a dying miner? Some in the Camborne community evidently suspected so. Is there evidence here of a cover-up?

An unwillingness to open fully matters of life and death in Camborne becomes further apparent later at this Local Board meeting. Back in 1881, there had been tension between the Medical Officer for Health and some Board members when E.S. Angrove, the Medical Officer, clashed with Captain Charles Thomas (see above, pp. 52-56). Now, in 1893, Dr. Erskine is the Medical Officer and once again there is a clash between competing structures of feeling, different ways of seeing the world. *The Cornish Telegraph* report has a section with the heading: '*THE MEDICAL OFFICER SEEKS FURTHER INFORMATION*'. Imagine the scene as Dr. Erskine stands and speaks: "*I wrote to the Clerk last December to ask him whether there were any reasons why the appointed Inspector [the surveyor and mining captain, T. Negus, who was also present at the meeting] should not furnish me with particulars as to the number of houses in the Board's district, the rooms the houses contained, and the number of inhabitants in each house. I have received no reply and I am therefore unable to send the required returns to the chairman of the Sanitary Committee of the County Council as I am obliged to do.*"

Mr. Josiah Rowe rose immediately and spoke: "*I think it is time for we local authorities to – how shall I express it? – to put our foot down! If we reply to all the communications that we get from Mr. Trevail, acting for Cornwall County Council, we will need to keep a special staff of clerks.*"

Someone laughed, and the Clerk himself, Mr. John R. Daniell, rose: "*Let me be clear: I should not be expected to give all these particulars. To do so for Camborne would be bad enough, but there are all the surrounding areas too. No – what matters is that we have been doing all we can to improve the town.*"

There are cries of "*Hear, hear*". The Clerk, encouraged, continued: "*There was a time when we had a death rate of 28 in the 1,000 per annum, but we have improved. The laying on of a proper supply of water has done a great deal, but make no mistake, our work as the Local Board has been very important, too. If we were to supply Mr. Trevail and the County Council with every bit of information that we possess, well – the fact is, it might be published and that could be to our detriment. That would be a great mistake.*"

More cries of "*Hear, hear*". Josiah Rowe rose again. "*The local authorities of this county of Cornwall have been long-suffering where Mr. Trevail is concerned. The demands that are being made of us are inconsistent.*"

There is the sound of disagreement in the room. Frederick Thomas, in the Chair, called "*Order, order*". Another member of the Board, Mr. W.H. Bunt (a County Councillor), reiterated the Board's obligation to provide the information requested, insisting that Mr. Trevail had done and is doing a good job in the interests of the county.

The Clerk rose again: "*I of course agree with every word that has fallen from Mr. Bunt. I told the Inspector that if he considered that the passing on of any information he might gather would not be prejudicial to the interests of this Board, he should continue to try to carry out his instructions.*"

Mr. A. Dunkin was on his feet. "*Let us be very clear. The working men's houses here in Camborne compare very favourably with the houses you find in the courts and alleys of Truro and Penzance!*"

Dr. Erskine had heard enough: "*It is your duty to improve the sanitary condition of the district in every possible way. I wanted to find out the sanitary conditions under which our poor lived, so that we might remedy an existing evil as far as possible—*"

Dunkin interrupted. "*But we can manage to remedy the evil – if it exists – without publishing it to the world.*"

"*Who said it was to be published?*" Erskine snapped back.

Captain Charles Thomas Junior was rising slowly to his feet. The room fell silent. "*We do not want all our defects to be published by Mr. Trevail. Penzance has a very strong feeling about that gentleman's actions.*" The Captain paused; his tone became more conciliatory. "*If we have brought his name forward, as Mr. Bunt complains we have, it has only been done because he was the person who wrote to us.*"

Cries of "*Hear, here*" rose from a section of the room. The Captain continued. "*We are doing the best we possibly can. And it is necessary to keep our information to ourselves.*"

Dunkin was back on his feet. "*Yes! Quite right. Let us keep our own counsel. I suspect all this fuss is because Dr Erskine and the Inspector don't see eye-to-eye.*"

"*Not at all!*", the doctor snapped back.

The Cornish Telegraph report, at that point, simply concludes: '*The subject then dropped.*'

Within a year, the days of Local Boards of Health such as Camborne were over, replaced by urban districts (see above, p. 53). The reasons why such Local Boards came to be regarded as no longer fit for purpose are evident in the scene from the vestry room in Camborne, depicted above. Defensiveness, bordering on paranoia; parochialism, rooted in an almost feudal attachment to territory; self-centredness, apparent in the performances of so many of the few allowed into public office; and a fear of public scrutiny, accompanied by a tendency to cover up the cracks.

These were the characteristics that made good local government difficult in Camborne and elsewhere. They are also, I suggest, the character-faults of many mine owners, shareholders, and managers. Such faults made mining disasters more likely.

Rest in peace, the seven men of Camborne and district who perished, entombed in the Dolcoath mine.

THE POOR MEN AND WOMEN AND CHILDREN OF CAMBORNE TAKE TO THE STREETS - THE RIOT OF 7th/8th OCTOBER 1873

S ources:
The Cornish Telegraph – **Wednesday 8 October 1873:**

DESPERATE RIOT IN CAMBORNE
GREAT EXCITEMENT AGAINST THE POLICE
EXTRA POLICE CALLED OUT
POLICEMEN STONED AND INJURED, GLASS BROKEN
PUBLIC HOUSES CLOSED
THE MILITARY TELEGRAPHED

Circumstances occurred yesterday (Tuesday) at Camborne without parallel since the new police system came into vogue… We question in fact, if the bread riots, of nearly 30 years ago, produced anything like the consternation and dismay which prevailed at Camborne throughout yesterday.

The Cornish Telegraph – Wednesday 15 October 1873:

Around three o'clock in the afternoon [Thursday 9 October] P.C. Burton, with another constable, visited the principal tradesmen of the town, and gave them notice to appear at the Assembly Rooms at 4 o'clock to be sworn in as special constables. Colonel Gilbert determined to pour in an extra force of police, and Mr. Miller (the predecessor of Sup. Stephens) was sent for. About 4 o'clock 35 persons were sworn in.

Mr. Thomas Bishop, mercer, then presented a petition to the chairman of the magistrates (Mr. W. Bickford-Smith), signed by himself and sixteen tradesmen, stating that:

'From time to time, and especially recently, reports have been currently circulated that the police in this neighbourhood, under the superintendence of Mr. Stephens, have been unnecessarily harsh in their dealings with persons; that they have apprehended persons when a summons would have been amply sufficient; and lastly, the public are led to believe that some prisoners have been improperly dealt with after being conveyed to the police station. We believe that some of the charges can be partially, if not wholly, substantiated; and we are therefore very strongly of opinion that an inquiry should be made as soon as practicable into the whole of the circumstances.'

[The next day, Friday 10 October] the magistrates assembled at 11 o'clock in the town hall, with its three riddled windows; there being present Capt. W. Bickford-Smith in the chair, and W. Harvey and G.L. Basset, Esqs. Col. Gilbert, the chief constable, was also present.

A batch of 28 of the leading merchants, tradesmen, mine-captains, &c., of the parish were sworn in as special constables for one month, with instructions to proceed instantly, in case of any outbreak, to the police station in Moor Street and await the orders of the chief constable or his representative. Three of the summoned inhabitants produced medical certificates of inability to serve as special constables and were excused.

Capt. Joseph Vivian, jun., said he supposed he must be sworn, but he took the oath with considerable reluctance. There was a dreadful bad feeling amongst the miners, and it would tend to their leaving the neighbourhood. Their migration was bad enough now – indeed men were going away as fast as they could – and these arrests would drive them away faster than ever.

[…]

And [at the trial of Elizabeth Bennetts, accused of robbery from the house of her neighbours, the Wearnes, less than a month before the riot] Mr. Wearne's eldest little one, left at home on the night of the robbery, said she saw someone pass through her bedroom; she called "Da, da!" but no one answered, and "a great boy went downstairs." This story was enough to secure the acquittal of Mrs. Bennetts and did so [on Friday 3 October 1873].

What was there in all this [the arrest and trial of Elizabeth Bennetts, the wife of a warehouseman who was also a Primitive Methodist lay preacher] to create ill feeling? The strict confinement, the refusal to take bail, the good characters of the accused and her husband, popular suspicion of other parties, and a rumour – we hope it is only a rumour – that the accused was subject to unnecessary actions in her cell, tending to harass and annoy, and to censure and misrepresentation, in order to extort a confession, and also that she was so visibly and distressingly ill when she walked from the station-house to the town hall throughout the inquiry which resulted in her discharge that a conveyance ought, in common humanity, to have been engaged to carry her to the town hall. Col. Gilbert pledged himself to the fullest and most impartial inquiry into the complaints of Mrs. Bennetts – complaints that he will hear from her himself. It is quite clear that all the neighbours of the innocent woman believe her story, and that its recital roused the feelings of sympathy with the sufferer and of indignation against the police which, eventually, led to tumult and violence.

The Royal Cornwall Gazette – **Saturday 18 October 1873:**

THE RIOT AT CAMBORNE
DISCHARGE OF THE PRISONERS
FULL PARTICULARS

In our report of the riotous proceedings at Camborne last week we showed that the affair wore a very different aspect from the ordinary riot which we read of in other parts of the country; in fact, that it was solely an outbreak against the arbitrary conduct of the police, and that there was no attempt whatsoever to destroy property or to interfere with the peaceable inhabitants, except in those few cases in which policemen had taken refuge in a house and the occupant refused the mob admission. The police were badly used, and the conduct of the mob cannot be in any way justified, though it may be explained; and it is to a certain extent satisfactory to know that the mining population are not animated by any hostility to the law or to the rights of property.

The proceedings before the magistrates during the week shews clearly that our estimate of the outbreak was the correct one, and that the people have much cause to complain of the manner in which the law has been enforced by Supt. Stephens and the police force under his charge. The antipathy to Stephens appears to have taken quite as strong a root in the minds of the tradesmen and shopkeepers of the town as in those of the working miners, which is forcibly shown by the fact that the Local Board has memorialised Col. Gilbert in favour of Stephen's removal, and of the substitution of Supt. Miller, who preceded Stephens at Camborne, and who, although an active and watchful officer, got on remarkably well with the people.

Evidence given at the trial of James Kent and Cornelius Burns, two men brought before the magistrates on Saturday October 11, 1873, and accused of being concerned in a riot:

"*Mr. John Mills: I am a builder and cabinet maker, carrying on business at Camborne. On Tuesday afternoon when the police made the sortie, I was standing at Pollard's corner, and saw Kent there. He was standing perfectly quiet and taking no part whatever in the riot. I also saw him knocked down by an elderly police officer, who appeared to me to be in charge of the other constables. The officer struck him on the head twice with his staff, and my impression at once was that he had made a mistake and hit the wrong person. I do not, however, wish to reflect upon the officer in any way because I believe he thought he was doing his duty.*"

Inspector Pappin denied that he struck a blow for the day.

The County and Borough Police Act 1856 was an Act of Parliament which made it compulsory for a police force to be established in any county which had not previously formed a constabulary. The establishment of the 'new police' that had begun in the 1820s with Robert Peel's penal, police, and law reforms was now a movement that covered the whole nation. The purpose of such police forces was to ensure that public order was maintained, and to this end, following the pattern elsewhere, a Watch Committee was formed in Camborne from 1857. Its members were drawn from those men who locally held a measure of wealth and power; its purpose was to oversee the local police force and keep an eye on matters of law and order.

As I argue in my doctoral thesis, *Drink in Victorian Norwich* (2003), the shadow of the French Revolution at the end of the eighteenth century fell over much of the next century too; the poor in 1789 had risen against those above them in the social hierarchy – and might conceivably do so in Britain. One effect of the Industrial Revolution had been to concentrate more people than ever before in urban centres. Most people in towns and cities were poor. At times of economic crisis, as relations between capital and labour became strained, the anxieties of the powerful and wealthy rose – at Westminster and at the level of urban or county politics. Norwich was no exception. Neither was Camborne.

By 1873, the public disorder associated with the bread riots in October 1847 across Cornwall, including Wadebridge, Camelford, St Austell, Redruth, Pool, Helston and Penzance, was a distant memory, as noted in the first source above.[26]

Despite the increases in population at times of mining

---

26 For more detail of these clashes between labour (the hungry poor) and capital (the local elites) in 1847, see The Cornish Historian (an online blog researched and written by Francis Edwards, a Camborne local historian) at https://the-cornish-historian.com

prosperity over the previous thirty years, Camborne had remained a town that enjoyed social stability. However, the fall in the price of tin, the consequent closure of some mining ventures, and the increase in the rate of migration of miners in search of work overseas (see above, pp. 21-23) had led to a degree of nervousness on the part of those whose capital or means of income was tied up in mining – see the testimony of Capt. Joseph Vivian Junior in the second source above. The last thing the urban elite needed in Camborne in these circumstances was a police force that had gone rogue under the leadership of its superintendent, Alfred Stephens. He was in 1873 a married man of forty-six years, originally from Newport on the Isle of Wight, who had been appointed to the constabulary in Liskeard in 1857 and promoted to superintendent in the Penzance borough in 1868. By 1873, Camborne would have experienced his style of police leadership for five years. The rioting over two days in Camborne in October 1873 was the direct consequence of such policing. The urban elite in a town in Great Britain suffered a breakdown in law and order for the best part of twenty-four hours as bands of miners and their families took control, the only restraining influence being the self-discipline of the mining community itself. This was an extraordinary event.

The Penzance Borough police force had had its headquarters at Camborne in Moor Street since 1835, the force comprising seven men. This Camborne focus was presumably in response to the concentration of miners and their families in that town and surrounding areas; in 1841, the Camborne population had been around 10,000; in 1873, just under 15,000. Once the Cornwall County Constabulary had been formed in 1857, the police presence grew with Camborne remaining the headquarters of the Penzance Borough force. Stephens was, as it turned out, the ill-chosen and in time widely hated successor to Henry Miller, who had served as the superintendent in Camborne between 1857 and 1868 before being transferred to head the force in the borough of Launceston. Henry Miller was the son of a labourer; all the members of Victorian police forces were working class in origin, but some evidently came to see their former peers as the enemy. The provision of a uniform and the power to take actions that could send men and women to gaol turned their heads. They became corrupt.

It was plain to many in the urban elite that the public disorder which led to the arrival of the military around twenty-two hours after the first stones were thrown was due to the actions of its own police. That force had been created more than a generation before to ensure the peace was kept, not provoke a riot. As Francis Edwards notes in his admirable blogpost (see above) on the Camborne riots, to which I am much indebted, all the Camborne police were either forced to resign shortly after the riots or were moved to other Cornish boroughs. Alfred Stephens was sacked within two days of the collapse of public order. The rioters had forced him to flee the town in a carriage, heading west, never to return. Henry Miller, now aged forty-nine, was persuaded to return to his old position where he remained for another seven years. There must have been a collective sigh of relief from all classes within Camborne and neighbouring areas at the return of a safe pair of hands.

How had it come to the point where rioting became the last resort of the whole mining community - men, women, and children - to right the wrongs they were suffering? Ill feeling between miners and police was becoming more common. It is evident in 1872 when two Camborne men, Alfred Rule, a single twenty-two-year-old tin dresser, and Thomas Phillips, a single twenty-four-year-old tin miner, were convicted of assaulting the police on duty in Camborne and sentenced to hard labour in Bodmin Gaol. Rule's employment in gaol was the treadmill; Phillip's was the treadmill and cooking.

The prison treadmill had been introduced nationally in 1818 to teach offenders the 'habits of industry.' At first, it was intended to be pointless and to punish; resistance to the motion of the treadmill was provided by straps and weights. Later, it became acceptable to use the energy produced to grind grain. By the Prison Act of 1865, every male prisoner over sixteen sentenced to hard labour had to spend at least three months of his sentence in so-called Labour Order, usually on the treadmill. The use of treadmills in prisons was abolished in 1902, the last year of Victoria's reign, following the Prison Act of 1898.

These two young miners experienced three months or more on the treadmill for a conviction of assault based on testimony from a police force that was increasingly seen by miners as hostile.

Further grounds for a breakdown of trust between the police force and the Camborne community of miners and their families, together with tradespeople, came a little over a week before the riot with the arrest, charging, and detention of Elizabeth Bennetts (misnamed as Rebecca Bennetts in *The Cornish Telegraph's* report at the time). *The Cornish Telegraph* edition for 15 October 1873 carried a piece by its reporter which explained that Bennetts, aged '*about 30*' and of good

Treadmill at Pentonville Prison – 1895.[27]

character, was the wife of a *'warehouseman named Bennetts'* (Thomas Bennetts) who was highly thought of by his *'master'*, and evidently by others in the Camborne community since he was *'a Primitive Methodist local preacher.'* Thomas and Elizabeth had married in 1869 and by the autumn of 1873 had four children, the youngest only eight weeks old at the time of her arrest.

Their neighbours in Stray Park Lane in Camborne, the Wearnes, had gone to market and whilst they were away fifteen sovereigns were stolen from a drawer in their bedroom by an intruder. The Camborne police, under Superintendent Stephens' direction, investigated and arrested Elizabeth

---

27   Source: Wikipedia image

Bennetts, confining her to gaol and then creating the grounds for rumour and speculation. Bennetts was innocent and acquitted on Friday 3 October 1873, as reported in *The Cornish Telegraph*, following the evidence of one of the Wearne's children – see the second source above. Why had the investigation by Stephens and his team not taken note of such evidence? Was it incompetence? Or malice? Or a combination of both?

The Royal Cornwall Gazette for Saturday 18 October 1873 provides a transcript of the interview between Colonel Walter Raleigh Gilbert (1813-1896), the inaugural Chief Constable for Cornwall from 1857-1896, and Elizabeth Bennetts, in which she makes her formal complaint regarding her treatment by the Camborne Police. Imagine the scene in the crowded Magistrates' Hall on Wednesday 15 October 1873. Colonel Gilbert has opened the inquiry, insisting that he had never received a complaint against the police without sifting the matter thoroughly.

Colonel Walter Raleigh Gilbert (1813-1896), the inaugural Chief Constable of Cornwall from 1857-1896[28]

---

28   Source: This image is used with the kind permission of the website, British Police History. See: https://british-police-history.uk

Elizabeth Bennetts' testimony:

"*P.C. Burton used to come to my cell at midnight and tell me that I had been seen going into the Wearne's home and that Tom, my husband, had told him that I had spent £9 or £10 between Saturday and Wednesday. When I asked Tom, he said he had said nothing of the sort.*

"*Burton said that I had better confess, as I had been seen committing the robbery. I said to him that I would not confess to anything. I was innocent. I would swear it on my life – and I am not long for this world you are making me so scared. Burton replied: 'We have twelve witnesses against you.'*

"*Tom, my husband, saw Dr. Butlin and said he needed to come to attend me, and he did, and he was on the point of saying something to me when Superintendent Stephens who was in the cell interrupted and said to the doctor not to ask me anything because otherwise I would be singing out for the doctor time and time again.*

"*Dr. Butlin then left and sometime afterwards Dr. Harris came to see me. He said I was not suffering from any disease, but I was very weak, and I needed rousing up and I should be given something to read because my brain had been affected a little. And I needed a proper bed which the police promised him I would have – but they did not keep their word.*

"*When I was first taken to the police station, I was searched by two women, and six days later they repeated that search. Two days after I was locked up,*

P.C. Burton accused me of throwing money into the closet in the cell, and I was removed to another cell while they did their search and had the closet cleaned out. That night, he came to my cell and asked again what I had thrown into the closet. I said: 'I've told your wife about you!' He pressed me again to answer his question and I told him again that I had told his wife. I burst out 'You will be the death of me if you keep harassing me. Do you visit all your prisoners at midnight?' He smiled and said 'Yes, we are expected to visit all our prisoners at midnight.'

"The next night, another constable, P.C. Nicholls, came to my cell at twenty minutes to twelve o'clock and asked 'Are you the landlady, Mrs ?' All I could do was answer 'No.' They knew who I was.

"During that time behind bars, they made me walk to the village of Trevenson, a mile and a half away, twice. And then I had to walk to the courthouse."

Other testimony delivered before Colonel Gilbert on that Wednesday 15 October 1873 in the Magistrates' Hall:

Colonel Gilbert then heard from others who 'wished to set the record straight regarding police conduct.' They included:

Captain S. Williams, a mine agent:

"I want to speak regarding the striking of Inspector Pappin. To the best of my eyesight, I saw the Inspector strike a man and the blood came issuing from the wound. Many others saw the same thing."

William Thomas, a miner:

"On Tuesday 7 October at five o'clock in the evening I was in Abraham's Hotel, and I saw Inspector Pappin coming towards the hotel. He left the constables that were with him, and I distinctly saw him strike a man over the head twice or three times. The man was taken into the hotel and given some brandy. He then walked out and towards the constables before collapsing on the ground."

Henry Jarves, a miner:

"About two weeks ago I was going home with my wife, in the company of Henry Yeo and his wife, when P.C. Bartlett threatened to lock me up. I had done nothing. I was simply standing up. Bartlett said if I did not move on, he would let me have it. I had been there then about two minutes. I am telling you this to show you the attitude of these policemen towards the people of Camborne. Bartlett was trying to excite me and my companions, and if we had drunk a beer or two more, there probably would have been a row."

John Miners, a miner:

"Eighteen months ago, the marionettes [puppet show performers] were at Camborne and I took my son to see them. He paid for a sixpenny place to see the show, but a dispute arose about whether my son had paid. The police got involved and I was taken in charge and brought before the magistrate. The police swore that I *was drunk and disorderly, and I was fined 19 shillings, including costs. It was P.C. Scantlebury who dragged me away. On the Sunday afterwards, the marionette man came to see me and said the police had no business to take my son into custody as he had not been charged. He and the other puppet show people felt so strongly about this injustice they would pay the fine, whatever it might be, and they did."*

The Royal Cornwall Gazette noted that all the statements of the witnesses were received with applause, and at the end of the inquiry Colonel Gilbert acknowledged that if the evidence he had heard were true, the police had certainly exceeded their duty which would be the last thing he wanted. He concluded: *"My hope for the future is that we can all now get on better since we have a new lot of policemen."* Those words were greeted with great applause.

The testimony above of Williams, the mine agent, and Thomas, the miner, suggests that Inspector George Pappin was lying when he claimed that he had not struck James Kent. The Camborne police force were evidently suffering from an institutional malaise in which no one dared break ranks and lying was endemic. Pappin must have calculated he could lie with impunity.

The Royal Cornwall Gazette for Saturday 18 October also references the trial of James Kent and another young miner, Cornelius Burns, on Saturday 11 October a few days after the riot – see the third source above. They faced charges of stone-throwing and being concerned in a riot, along with a third young man, James Bryant, who was arrested later in the depths of the Dolcoath mine where he worked. They were and remained the only men arrested in the aftermath of the riot. Bryant joined Kent and Burns in the dock on that Saturday. A short while later, he was a free man. He had been at the 230 fathom in Dolcoath until 6 pm, and was at home from then until going to bed at 9.30 pm. There was no case to answer and he was discharged.

The only witness who thought she perhaps had seen Bryant was the innkeeper's wife, whose public house had been damaged in the riot as the mob hunted for hidden policemen. She was clearly bearing grudges. All the other witnesses – a mine agent, a mine broker, a mine purser, a surgeon, a doctor, a grocer, a bank manager, and an accountant – did as the police force had done. They did not break ranks. No one could identify any rioter. One or two names did slip out, but they had all left town the day after the riot. Indeed, it was now generally agreed that it had been children who were the stone-throwers, for the most part. The magistrates had no choice but to retire – for less than an hour – and return to discharge Kent and Burns too.

The bench of magistrates – which included Gustavus Basset, the lord of Tehidy and owner of the Dolcoath mine – would have understood that the wall of silence concerning the identity of any actual rioter was a prearrangement. The three men in the dock seem to have been chosen because their observed actions meant they would not be convicted of rioting. Captain Josiah Thomas, the senior mine captain at Dolcoath, having been sworn in as a special constable was one of those who arrested Bryant in the depths of the mine. Thomas must have known he was arresting a man with an alibi. These were motions to be gone through; judicial proceedings had to be carried out; the eyes of Westminster and the Home Secretary, Robert Lowe, might be turned in their direction.

The magistrates expressed the appropriate sentiments, as they rounded off proceedings: "*The Bench was sorry to observe the unwillingness of all classes to furnish information as to the real offenders, but we hope that others will come forward to assist in the detection and punishment of the rioters.*"

But, in truth, it suited the great and the good and all the classes in Camborne that a line should be drawn under this unfortunate incident. No rioters were detected and punished. All was best buried and forgotten. In the eyes of the urban elite and the middle class in Camborne, the mining workforce was too precious a commodity to have them suffer any retribution for their law-breaking. Captain Joseph Vivian Junior, as noted above in the second source, took the oath to become a special constable on Friday 10 October with considerable reluctance. There was, as he said, now such bad feelings within the mining community that even more of them would take the migration route if a policy of arresting them was followed.

Here was a man of standing in the community unafraid to tell the truth, to identify the elephant in the room: in effect, the dependence of capital upon labour. Mr. T. Cornish, the clerk to the magistrates, now reminded Captain Vivian that there were still matters of procedure to be observed. Here was a nudge to remind Vivian that the urban elite could not afford to be seen, or heard, siding with the miners. The chair of the magistrates was Captain William Bickford-Smith (1827-99), a Justice of the Peace for Cornwall whose captaincy was military; it was not a mining title. He was the grandson of the inventor of the safety fuse and a partner in

Bickford, Smith & Co, a fuse-making factory in Tuckingmill outside Camborne, with markets across the world.

Mr. Cornish, with some impatience: "*That is no reason why you should not be sworn to assist in the preservation of the peace.*"

Capt. Vivian: "*But I say the whole proceeding is unnecessary. The police have been most arbitrary in the discharge of their duties. How is it—*"

Captain Bickford-Smith, from the Chair, interrupted: "*What is the object of your address?*"

Capt. Vivian: "*The object of it is to justify my dislike to taking this oath, and to state that I do it under protest – in fact I would not do it at all were I not compelled to.*"

Mr. Cornish, even more impatiently: "*But you are compelled to. As to the police, were you not in court yesterday when Col. Gilbert promised the fullest inquiry into their conduct?*"

Capt. Vivian: "*No. But Burton and Stephens have done all this mischief. Burton was drummed out of the parish he left to come here, and there is not a man more disliked in the world than Stephens.*"

Capt. Bickford-Smith: "*Are you prepared to make any specific charge against anyone?*"

Captain Vivian: "*Only this – one of the most respectable inhabitants of St Germans [a village and parish in East Cornwall, within the police division of Liskeard] told me that Burton was drummed out of that parish.*"

Capt. Bickford-Smith: "*I don't think that has anything to do with our efforts to preserve the peace in Camborne, or that we can recognise what has taken place elsewhere.*"

Capt. Vivian: "*I think it has a great deal to do with it.*"

The Cornish Telegraph ad verbatim report of this opening to proceedings next states simply, '*Capt. Vivian was then sworn.*'

The urban elite were united in their determination to deal with this riot in a way that minimised any damage to their control over their workforce of miners. Captain Vivian wanted that outcome too, but he did not take kindly to being told not to stir the waters by naming names in a public court. He disliked such prohibitions, still observable years later in the vestry room in Camborne in the Local Board meeting in 1893 (see above, p.97). However, as Captain Vivian's experience confirms, a fear of public scrutiny, accompanied by a tendency to cover up the cracks, was deeply ingrained in the social fabric.

Still, Captain Vivian had given voice to what everyone was saying. Superintendent Stephens and P.C. Burton were at the core of the rottenness in the local police force. Their removal was rapid. Stephens was formally dismissed on 12 October 1873; Burton was forced to resign on 21 October 1873. Yet they faced no criminal proceedings. All was, as noted above, best buried and forgotten. But how serious and damaging are the actions of rogue individuals. The Camborne riot that occurred in response to such actions could have led to deaths and, with those fatalities, considerable notoriety, and national attention.

Elizabeth Bennetts' treatment by PC Burton has been examined above. Those actions helped light the fuse that led to the riot. Burton's further actions helped produce the explosion of anger that sent around three thousand miners and their families on to the streets of Camborne in unprecedented riot on Tuesday 7 October 1873. In the edition for Wednesday 15 October, *The Cornish Telegraph's* reporter provides an account of the build-up to the riot and the role of P.C. Burton, who was a single 26-year-old labourer from St Breock in north Cornwall when he was appointed in 1862 and stationed in Liskeard. He was transferred to the Penzance force in Camborne in 1868, the same year that Superintendent Stephens arrived in Camborne. Burton, aged thirty-seven in 1873, '*was looked upon as his (Stephens) right-hand man*', in the words of the newspaper report.

When there was trouble outside the Market House around 6.30 pm on Saturday 4 October, the countdown to the riot started. Tempers flared between P.C. James Osborne and James Bawden, a thirty-year-old miner, a reputedly '*decent and hard-working lad.*' Several eyewitnesses later contradicted P.C. Osborne's statement that Bawden had pushed him and then aimed a kick. As P.C. Osborne tried to collar Bawden, P.C. Harris arrived on the scene, as did Joseph Bawden, the twenty-six-year-old brother of James, and also a miner. A scuffle broke out in which the unarmed Bawden brothers gave as good as they got and made their escape, aided, according to P.C. Osborne, '*by 400 and 500 locals.*' Such an estimate of supporters seems most unlikely. Osborne and Harris had been humiliated in a fight by two miners; they were not going to admit that. At 10.30 pm that evening, P.Cs Osborne, Harris, Burton, Bartlett and Nicholls arrived at the Bawdens' home in Trelowarren Street, which led to them being arrested and taken to the police station, kicking, and struggling. It was what happened next at the police station that triggered the fury of the estimated three thousand who took to the streets.

Whatever the later police denials, people believed the testimony of a local who was resident close by. Anthony Cock was a respected member of the community, living in Moor Street where the police station was situated. *The Royal Cornwall Gazette* edition for Saturday October 11, 1873, noted that Cock:

'...*has a reputation for being a good man whom no amount of pressure could induce to tell a lie. He devotes a good deal of his time to visiting the families of the poorer miners and affording them all the assistance and consolation in his power, and they have, one and all, the greatest possible faith in his integrity.*'

According to Anthony Cock, and others passing by, in their sworn statements before the magistrates, they heard '*screeches of* "*Murder*"' from the station, and a policeman say, "*Give it to the buggers!*" Was that the voice of Stephens? Or Burton? Or another police officer? Then a police staff was lifted, one of the prisoners was struck, and screamed "*Murder!*"

By the time the Bawden brothers were brought to trial in the Court House within the Town Hall, on Tuesday 7 October, the anger in the town was at boiling point. More police had been brought in from other divisions in Cornwall as a precaution. *The Cornish Telegraph* report on 15 October notes that:

'...*the scene outside [the Court House] among the excited assemblage baffles description. There was an incessant hubbub and noise – a seething of the cauldron soon to boil over. The angry populace told and retold the stories of the wrongs at official hands of Mrs. Bennetts, the Bawdens, and others.'*

Captain Bickford-Smith was hit by a stone whilst aiding and shielding the police. It had, apparently, been intended for P.C. Harris. When Superintendent Stephens appeared at the front door of the Town Hall, there was such a yell and a discharge of stones, *'hastily kicked up from the macadamised road.'* Inside the Court House, the Bawden brothers were subject to a trial of some three and a half hours. At its conclusion, they were found guilty of assault, and both sentenced to five months on the treadmill in Bodmin gaol. The problem for the authorities now was how to get them out and forward them to that prison. At 4 pm, the doors of the Town Hall were opened and around a half-dozen police constables stormed out, with staves raised, to join their fellow officers outside and attack the gathered mob. It was a feint. The Bawden brothers were slipped out, in handcuffs, from the rear of the Town Hall and driven in a carriage to Bodmin gaol under the supervision of Colonel Gilbert.

Whether the Colonel should have left the scene was debated by others later, but he must have felt that only his presence could avert the forcible release of the prisoners if the carriage was intercepted by rioters. By the evening, he was back in Camborne, having delivered the two miners to their prison, and no doubt in discussion with Bickford-Smith about the appropriate response to this unprecedented loss of social control. According to *The West Briton and Cornwall Advertiser* on Thursday 9 October, a crowd of around three hundred approached Bickford-Smith's residence on Beacon Hill, near the railway station, late on

Tuesday night. But if the story is true, no militant action followed.

Back at the town hall, with the Colonel and the two convicted miners having departed, the police evacuated the building, the last man leaving around 5 pm. They tried to make their way through the rioters, with the help of their staves, to reach the Moor Street police station. With the police presence gone, the children of the miners, together with a group of bal maidens, now had their turn, smashing the windows of the Town Hall in a hail of stones, whilst their parents set about isolating and chasing individual policemen. It was in this riotous chaos that Inspector Pappin sustained his injury and Kent his. As *The West Briton and Cornwall Advertiser* edition for Thursday 9 October stated: '...*the whole town, was from about five o'clock in the afternoon until about four o'clock the following morning at the mercy of the mob.*'

P.C. Oliver's attempts to hide in a van were unsuccessful. He was dragged out and beaten, before finding sanctuary in the house of Walter Pike, a mine purser. Escaping later to the port of Hayle to the south, he was treated there by a doctor who, after examining the bruising to the back, legs, and shoulders, the lame leg, and the inflamed eyeball, offered the opinion that the man was lucky to be alive.

The local newspapers have stories of other policemen, at least seven, who were caught and beaten, along with accounts of those who did manage to evade their hunters, some with the help of local traders.

One policeman who did not escape on that Tuesday was P.C. Burton. He tried to leave the town on the Redruth-Helston carriage which stopped in Camborne, but the carriage was halted by the mob and Burton dragged out and beaten. He did somehow escape and made it as far as the Railway Inn, where he was rediscovered and subject to another beating by a different group of rioters. *The Royal Cornwall Gazette*, reporting on Saturday 11 October, said that Burton was badly beaten about the body and cut on the head. Yet, it is clear the miners' wrath stopped short of actual intent to murder. They were not going to hang for the likes of a man such as Burton, or Stephens if they had managed to catch him. Indeed, if *The Cornish Telegraph* report on Wednesday 15 October is correct, P.C. Burton had recovered enough to be back on duty by Thursday 9 October, visiting the principal tradesmen of the town with another constable to give them notice of their swearing-in as special constables (see above, p.99). Burton's dismissal from the force came on 21 October.

A group of the rioters had turned their attention to the police station in Moor Street from probably as early as 6 pm. Some thought the Bawden brothers might have been taken back there from the Town Hall.

The Cornish Telegraph for 15 October provides this account:

'*The outer wall of the yard was climbed, the double doors unfastened, and the superintendent's well-known light spring cart dragged out. In a twinkle the shafts were snapped off and the vehicle, after being drawn and tumbled the length of Trelowarren Street towards the Market House, was knocked up. Another party invaded the station in such numbers that the police were powerless... and gave up the keys. The seven constables and a sergeant present, with four women [including the wife of Stephens and the wife of Burton] were allowed safe passage by the mob whose prey was elsewhere. Their cry was 'Where's Stephens? Where's Burton, Bartlett, and Osborne? If we catch them, we'll murder them.'... Inside the prison... furniture was destroyed... the quest was for things belonging to the superintendent and the force. Coats were dismembered, hats flung into the street, a clock and watches put up to mock auction and, when sold, smashed. Every window was riddled.'*

Captain Bickford-Smith had bravely arrived at the police station and was given a hearing for some minutes, but the rioting miners refused his order to disperse. They were in control. A vigilance committee had been formed; the search for the most unpopular policemen was underway. Pubs where fugitive policemen were suspected to have hidden were ransacked and their windows smashed.

By dawn next day, the great and the good of Camborne must have been in deep conference. What should they do? By noon they had decided. The military authorities at Plymouth must be called in. A telegram arrived at the Davenport barracks at 12.30 on Wednesday morning; by 2.30 pm six commissioned officers, six sergeants, a hundred men, and two drummers of the 11th Foot were off by a special train from Plymouth station. At 4.30 pm, with no sign of a riot other than the debris and broken windows, the military force was marching from Camborne station to the drill-room. By 7.30 pm, Inspector Pappin, his head plastered and looking very much the invalid, was seen in conference with the commanding officer of the army unit.

On Wednesday evening, the town was now filled by people discussing the rioting of the previous day. Some condemned the action of police authorities, including Colonel Gilbert, in abandoning their men, and the inaction of the magistrates in not reading the Riot Act and straightaway calling out special constables. There were various rumours afloat about the conduct of the police in the case of Mrs. Bennetts. Some of the supposed ringleaders of the rioting mob were 'spotted' by plain-clothed police constables that evening, but none arrested. The miners and their families were, by and large, now absent from the scene. They must have sensed this was a time to lie low.

All-in-all, it had been a close call. For the best part of a day, the people who had wealth and power had had to bow to working class anger. Capital had been compelled to recognise the force of labour, albeit briefly. However, no lives had been lost. The glaziers would be busy fitting new panes of glass and a few premises, not least the police station, had been trashed, but the urban elite could breathe a huge sigh of relief and make the adjustments needed. By Thursday, Colonel Gilbert had increased the force of police in the town from around seven to fifty men, now under the command of Superintendent Miller. By Friday, the magistrates had sworn in around thirty special constables, the number later being increased to eighty, although at least one, Captain Joseph Vivian, had expressed his reluctance to be signed up for an exercise that he feared could lead to more arrests and serve as a provocation for the mining community.

However, the urban elite in Camborne knew what they were doing. The swearing-in of so many special constables from the ranks of the middle classes served as a political statement to those in the county and nation who were more powerful: '*We have the matter under control. You can leave it to us.*' And if the compulsory recruitment of special constables was for show, so too was the trial of the three miners arrested. The choice of these three men rather than others whose guilt was more likely to be proved, together with the wall of silence from witnesses and the consequent lack of evidence, led to their acquittal and discharge on Saturday. No further prosecutions followed. The two miners, the Bawden brothers, who clashed with P.Cs Osborne and Harris in the Market Square in the fracas that began the chain of events which led to the riot, were now walking the treadmill in Bodmin Gaol. So much the better. But as for the police force, Camborne needed rid of them, and new men brought in under the trusted control of Superintendent Miller brought back in his old role.

Colonel Gilbert, the Chief Constable, performed sterling work when he sat as Chair of the Inquiry into complaints against the police on the following Wednesday, the 15th of October, a week after the riot. Elizabeth Bennetts was able to make her statement of mistreatment, although she was likely to have still been traumatised by the experience. Her fourth child was still less than three months old, and she had been separated from her children for some time whilst in prison. Now she had become the talk of the town. Perhaps there was some healing for her in being able to speak at the inquiry. For the others, too, who gave their accounts of police misbehaviour, there would have been some sense of justice being done. However, the most important outcome of the inquiry for the urban elite was, in the telling words of Colonel Gilbert, that '*we can all now get on better since we have a new lot of policemen.'* Getting on together was an aspiration that could dissolve any notion of a struggle between capital and labour.

Perhaps, Colonel Gilbert's hope was well-founded. Deference and submissiveness were restored, up to a point. But it is likely that those who experienced such a riotous week in Camborne would have been changed by the experience. Radical politics did surface in the town between 1885 and 1895, when Charles Conybeare was the MP (see above, pp. 69-70). What remains indisputable is that for a day or two, the working class in Camborne overthrew an oppressive and brutal agency of social control – the local police force – and those who had power and wealth were forced to side with this outcome, through economic and moral necessity. The pursuit of profit from mining, together with Christian conscience, spelt an end to police thuggery.

It is extraordinary that this working class victory is not better known, understood, and celebrated. Where else in the nation during the Victorian period is there a similar example of such successful resistance to a power that had been abused?

A NEW CENTURY – THE WORKING CLASS DIE ON THE BATTLEFIELDS IN THE GREAT WAR (1914-1918)

S ources:
Cornish Guardian – **Friday 04 September 1914:**

LADY WARMINGTON'S RECRUITING CORPS FOR CORNWALL

OFFICIALLY AUTHORISED BY THE WAR OFFICE

[TO THE EDITOR]

Sir, – The War Office having authorised me to undertake a recruiting Campaign through Cornwall visiting – Bodmin, Camborne, Redruth, Helston, St Austell, Falmouth, Penzance, Launceston, Newquay, Truro, St Just, St Ives, and Wadebridge, may I through your valuable paper make an appeal to all in Cornwall for their personal help.

My plan is to have processions with music and to hold patriotic concerts and open air meetings at which speeches will be made to urge men to join Lord Kitchener's Army. I also propose to make a special appeal to the women to influence their men to serve their king and country.

Will anyone interested in this movement write to me – Co, Captain Harrison, recruiting officer, Bodmin.

ANNE WARMINGTON

Cornish Guardian – Friday 04 September 1914:

The following letter has also appeared in the daily papers:

Sir – I have read with hot anger Lady Maxwell's letter to the Press this morning.

To accuse the manhood of England of cowardice and skulking shows that she has failed to grasp the real reasons why so many are at present hanging behind. The real reason is the totally inadequate sum that is being paid to England's soldiers, and especially the Territorial units.

To leave a wife behind to live upon a paltry sum of approximately 15s a week, and in addition to this to know that life insurances are not payable on war risks, is sufficient to make the bravest hesitate. 15s will not even pay for the upkeep of decent homes, much less cover the food question. In the South African war [the Boer War, 1899-1902], there was no lack of volunteers, but in that case the Imperial Yeomanry was paid 7s per day.[29]

G.A. Brittain,
27 Waterloo Bridge, Aug.27, 1914

---

29   15s a week in 1914 = c.£82 today; 7s per day in 1900 = c.£350 a week today

Cornish Guardian – **Friday, 04 September 1914:**

What the War Means in Men

HOW LORD KITCHENER PROPOSES TO RAISE THE HUMAN MATERIAL FOR A LONG WAR

What the war will mean to this country is shown by a remarkable article in the "Times" by its military correspondent, in which he shows how Lord Kitchener is preparing for a long war.

The author says: '*We are fighting a nation of seventy million people and we have no good reason to suppose that they have any object in life but to crush us if they can... Behind the German lines are immense resources... In such conditions, the war may be long, very long... it is Lord Kitchener's duty to prepare our land forces so that... by their steadily expanding numbers and their constantly increasing efficiency we are enabled to play a part worthy of England in the war and at the peace impose terms most in consonance with our interests.*

'*At the base of Lord Kitchener's plans, therefore, lies this need for preparing for a long war and this further need, experienced by Chatham and Pitt, of steadily increasing our military power, day in day out and year by year, until at last... we may figure, in arms and manner, befitting the wealth and spirit of our Empire and the legacy of a great and honourable past.*

'*Lord Kitchener, therefore, may quite conceivably have to employ 500,000 additional men, and it is possible that when other Powers have exhausted themselves, we shall be, as we have been in the past, most capable of continuing the war.*

'There must be no negotiation of peace except on our terms.

'...No disasters must affright us... We are fighting for the liberties and even existence of Europe, and we must make the world know what it means to turn the thoughts of our people, and their stupendous energies, to war.'

The Cornishman – Wednesday 4 December 1918

CAMBORNE WAR PENSIONS COMMITTEE

Mr. J. Tabb, who presided over a meeting of the Camborne and District War Pensions Committee last week, congratulated the members of the Navy, Army, and Air forces on the magnificent victory won, but reminded the committee that their duties were by no means finished. Mr. Quintrell, the secretary, had 36 cases to bring forward that evening, and he knew the members of the committee could be relied upon to see that every discharged man, and the dependents of serving men received all the benefits the Government intended they should have. He thought a sufficient indemnity should be obtained from the central powers to meet the huge cost this country had been put to in connection with pensions to discharged men, and the dependents of those who had made the supreme sacrifice.

The Cornish Post and Mining News and Redruth Effective Advertiser – Saturday January 4 1919:

A BETTER NEW YEAR

An editorial from Herbert Thomas (1866-1951), the proprietor of the newspaper

With the advent of 1919, I am reminded that it was in 1889 – thirty years ago this Spring – that I turned my back on California and began my pilgrimage back to Cornwall... my birthplace. [Herbert Thomas spent seven years in Cornish mining offices before emigrating to California in 1887 to work as a reporter and interviewer for the San Francisco Daily Examiner. *Two years later, he returned and joined the staff of* The Cornishman. *In 1895, he became the managing editor of the* Cornish Post and Mining News *and its proprietor. In 1903, he sold the* Post *to the Cornishman Newspaper Company Ltd for shares and became managing editor of both papers. In 1908, he obtained control of* The Cornish Telegraph *and* The Cornish Tidings *and became the managing editor of the four newspapers.]*

...I little thought what wonderful and beautiful and terrible things would be crowded into the thirty years, which end with a benign, somewhat stubborn, somewhat hopeful journalist looking out from his newspaper pulpit, glad to be alive, in spite of the knowledge that "The Spectator" writer was right when he said recently that any middle-aged man, who saw a youth maimed or legless, ought to be ashamed that he is still alive and untouched by the war. I know that we middle-aged men ought

to have stopped the bullets, but the World is not a world of even-handed justice... When I read of the ex-Kaiser in Holland shooting game for recreation; when I talk with boys from my newspaper office who have come back with wounds from France and Italy, or from imprisonment in Germany; when I read the letters and Christmas greetings some of them send me, I simply feel amazed at the topsy-turveydom of things. You can talk to me until the sky falls about the divine purpose running through the world war which has slain at least ten million men in the pride of life; I can neither follow you understandingly, nor dogmatise to the contrary.

I look out from my newspaper pulpit and say: 'Well, my dears, it is a bad business; we neither desired it nor courted it... We must begin all over again, hoping that good will come out of evil; that we shall have learnt something from the struggle and suffering, and that time will prove there is still more good than evil...

...If we can only get "a Heaven of clean toil" on earth it will help to atone for the great crime of the war itself. Anyhow, my dears, may 1919 bring you less misery and more happiness than 1918.

Richard Van Emden and Harry Patch (2007), *The Last Fighting Tommy*:

[Harry Patch, 1898-2009, was born in Somerset and died when he was 111 years old. Aged eighteen, he was called up to fight in October 1916 and joined the 7th Duke of Cornwall Light Infantry. By this time, the regimental losses had been such that it was the norm for new recruits not to be from

Cornwall. He was a reluctant conscript who nevertheless did his duty and served as a machine-gunner in the trenches for four months near Ypres in the battle of Passchendaele in 1917. He was badly wounded by shrapnel in September 1917 and sent back to Britain. Harry Patch never spoke of his war experiences until he had reached the age of one hundred. Only then did he begin sharing his memories. The following extracts are from the book he wrote with the historian and writer, Richard Van Emden.]

'I had no inclination to fight anybody. I mean, why should I go out and kill somebody I never knew, and for what reason? I wasn't at all patriotic. I went and did what was asked of me and no more...

'The [Lewis machine gun] team was very close-knit and it had a pact. It was this: Bob [the no. 1 on the gun] said we wouldn't kill, not if we could help it. He said, "We fire short, have them in the legs, or fire over their heads, but not to kill, not unless it's them or us."

'We now waited for the whistle to blow [before advancing over the top of the trench towards the German lines]... It was just shell holes, and the team made its way forward in a line. It was absolutely sickening to see your own dead and wounded, some calling for stretcher bearers, others semi-conscious and beyond all help, and the German wounded lying about too, and you couldn't stop to help them. I saw one German – I should think he'd been dead some time – well, a shell had hit him and all his side and back were ripped up, and his stomach was out on the floor, a horrible sight. Others were just blown to pieces; it wasn't a case of seeing them with a nice bullet hole in their tunic, far from it, and there I was, only nineteen years old. I felt sick...

'We were reviewed on one occasion by a senior officer. I thought it was the King, but I must be wrong. I remember being reviewed only because the officers and NCOs had a hell of a job to get us out to cheer him. We were too damned tired...

'Front-line service wore the men down. I would get a butterfly in my stomach and my hands would shake, so for a moment or two I would have a job to coordinate my nerves to do anything. You couldn't deal with the fear and apprehension we had about being hit by shrapnel. It was there and it always would be. I know the first time I went to the line we were scared; we were all scared...

'By the time I was demobbed I was thoroughly disillusioned. I could never understand why my country could call me from a peacetime job and train me to kill a man I never knew. Why did we fight? I asked myself that, many times. At the end of the war, the peace was settled round a table, so why couldn't they do that at the start, without losing millions of men? I left the army with my faith in the Church of England shattered... I didn't discuss the war with anyone from then on, and nobody brought it up if they could help it...

'Until that birthday [Harry Patch's 100th, in 1998] I wouldn't mention it [the Great War]. I didn't mention the war even to my first wife and we were together for fifty-seven years... I've been told that I'm the last survivor of the trenches, the last fighting Tommy; I like that title... Going back to France was nothing I ever thought I would do, and certainly not at 105 years old... but in the end, I don't know why, I decided to go and I am pleased that I did. Seeing Ypres again and the battlefields was very emotional... When I first went back I travelled with two other veterans, Jack Davis and Arthur Halestrap. Jack was Duke of Cornwall's Light Infantry as well, and we formed a bond.'

In my analysis of Victorian Cornish mining and its importance for Cornish communities, I made several deductions.

I suggested that, in the context of Mrs. Alexander's Victorian hymn with its division of society into rich and poor, high and lowly (see above, pp.39-42), it was not just the poor people's estate that was being ordered by Divine Providence, it was their fate. Regarding the men who went underground to mine, it was their destiny to either die young or live on in ill health, too sick to work, before dying in middle-age.

I also offered the opinion, after examining the lives of those who were the wealthiest and most powerful in the local Camborne community, that there was a link between the senseless slaughter of game birds bred to be killed and the maiming and early death of miners (see above, p.48). In Camborne, as elsewhere in Cornwall, the birds were shot within the estates of those landowners who were also the most powerful and richest mine owners. It was these land-owning families who controlled the flow of capital that kept the mines open. The game birds they shot were destined to die since they were an inferior species bred for the purpose of providing entertainment and diversion. A parallel can be drawn with the men who were paid to mine underground. The inferior status of such miners had obliged them to enter a contract which would likely lead to their early death. Such was the necessary, if regrettable, outcome of capitalising upon the natural resources that lay, by seeming good fortune, under the ground owned by a few rich families.

I further speculated that this endemic disregard for health and safety that is evident in the mining industry had fear at its roots. The owners of capital needed workers, but such labour had to be controlled. The memories of the French Revolution at the end of the eighteenth century remained a constant during much of the nineteenth century. The so-called lower orders could be dangerous, not least after such an exponential expansion in urban communities that followed the increase in population. Control through policing was one way to ensure a stable society, but the maintenance of deference and respect for the ordained order in society was also vital. The lower orders were different and potentially dangerous but if handled in the right way, they could continue to be an asset. The collective work of tin miners in Cornwall, after all, had at times produced extraordinary wealth for the few who owned capital.

Mine owners would have been afraid of losing money in their ventures. That was a fear they understood. There was however, I suggest, this other less than conscious fear: a fear of the many, whose lives were so different from those of the privileged few. In a pre-Freudian world, such a subtle feeling would have been largely unacknowledged. Yet it does help explain the disregard and contempt for the lives and welfare of most of the population (see above, pp.76-77). When hardship and suffering in your town and surrounding villages is so often evident, a mental barrier may well be needed to separate you from those who make you uncomfortable and stir up buried feelings of guilt and fear. So, miners got sick and died young because that was the way of the world. Accidents will happen in mines. This is not our fault, would have been the default position of the mine owners, given the structure of feeling that shaped their way of seeing the world. Liberal Christian reformers were working away to lay in place an alternative structure of feeling but the detail of my book to date suggests they had a fight on their hands.

It also seemed to me that there was a link between the senseless slaughter of game birds, the maiming and early death of miners, and the slaughter of around 9 million humans on the battlefields of the World War fought between 1914 and 1918. My focus now moves forwards to that so-called Great War, and I explore its impact in Cornwall in general and specifically in Camborne and its neighbouring regions, teasing out the links between the deaths of birds, miners, and those caught up in war.

The source material on page 128 above took me by surprise when I first discovered it. I knew that there was a contemporary meme circulating in the autumn of 1914 that the war would be over by Christmas. I did not realise that the length of what became 'The Great War' and, in time, 'The First World War', had been anticipated in advance by those with the responsibility for its leadership and conduct. These men were calculating and smart enough to be planning for a long war against Germany and the other Central Powers, the so-called Quadruple Alliance comprising the German Empire, the Austro-Hungarian Empire, the Ottoman (Turkish) Empire, and the Kingdom of Bulgaria. The members of the Triple Entente, that is the imperial powers of Britain, France, and Russia, were now in conflict with an alliance led by Kaiser Wilhelm's Germany, the nation of 'seventy million people' according to the source. In fact, the accepted population figures are 67 million within Germany and a further 10.7 million in the German colonies – a total approaching 78 million. The British population recorded in the 1911 census was just over 43 million. However, the population of the British Empire at the outbreak of war in 1914 was around 88 million; the British Empire was the largest imperial power the world had ever known and would provide the military manpower to help compensate for the relatively smaller population of Britain compared with Germany.

The population figures for the other powers that found themselves at war in 1914 reveal the extent of their potential manpower available for military purposes. The Austro-Hungarian Empire had 50.6 million; the Ottoman Empire 23 million. Within the Triple Entente, the French Empire had a population of 60 million people, which included around 40 million in France. The Russian Empire, which included Finland and Poland, had a population of around 166 million, of which 90 million were in Russia. In each of these countries at the outbreak of war, those in power set about the task of mobilising their young men for war. This was a war between imperial alliances that had developed because of competition for imperial power and prestige and, crucially, natural resources and markets. Indeed, all the countries at war would have been planning, as the British were, for a long period of combat in which many lives would be lost. They knew they had the population resources, that is, the young men – 'THE HUMAN MATERIAL FOR A LONG WAR', in the words of the *Cornish Guardian* headline – to sustain such an anticipated period of warfare.

Before returning to the Cornish perspective to examine the way in which young men were mobilised into the armed forces with the aim of wounding and killing their foes, it helps to grasp the multi-dimensional nature of this war. Cornish men and their families were being sucked into the vortex of an unprecedented war that would be fought on so many fronts. It is only too easy to slip into a parochial perspective in which the war becomes synonymous with the military action on the Western Front and so neglecting the significance of the Eastern and Balkan Fronts.

There was also the naval front. This was a sea war fought on the surface between fleets with massive firepower, with submarines operating below the surface. One of the critical moments in the war came after a German U-boat submarine torpedoed the British-owned steamship 'Lusitania', killing 1,195 people, including 128, Americans in May 1915 and so setting off a chain of events that led to the entry of the USA into the war in April 1917. American involvement on the Western Front was one of the key factors explaining the eventual surrender of the German High Command in November 1918.

The militarisation of so much of the youth of the world is simply staggering. It is almost too much to comprehend, as is the slaughter of so many of those young men in the years that followed. Tens of millions of young men were given, in Harry Patch's words, the command to go out and kill other men they didn't know. Many would have chosen, as Harry did, to shoot in ways that made killing less likely. Many might have shared Harry Patch's lack of patriotism. Few would have grasped that this was a knowingly long war, fought between imperial powers for control over resources and markets, which needed them as human material for battle.

The casualties in this Great War were far greater in number than in previous wars. A recent calculation is that around 8.5

million soldiers died of wounds and/or disease, although an accurate table of losses will never be possible. Most casualties were inflicted by artillery, followed by small arms, and then by poison gas. It was the application of new technologies, developed because of industrialisation, that created these killing fields. More powerful guns and shells and rifles and bullets, and the application of advances in the chemistry of gases, provided most of the dynamics for slaughter.

Soldiers from the Duke of Cornwall Light Infantry gathered beside a stranded British tank on the Western Front in 1916.[30]

When the Great War began in 1914, the Russian Empire had the largest standing army with around 1.4 million soldiers on duty. This Russian army bore the brunt of the fighting

30 Source: Bodmin Keep, Cornwall's Army Museum, who have given their kind permission for its use.

against the Central Powers on the Eastern Front, as well as being involved in the fighting on the Balkan Front and the Western Front. The French Empire had a standing army of around 761,000 with over 1.3 million trained reservists. The British Empire had a relatively small professional army of around 250,000 regular soldiers and a further 250,000 trained territorials, with another 200,000 reservists – around 700,000 trained soldiers in all.

On the other side, the German Empire had a standing army of 700,000 soldiers at the outbreak of war. Within a week, some 3.8 million men were under arms. By August 1916, around 2.85 million German soldiers were serving on the Western Front, with a further 1.7 million in action on the Eastern Front. The Austro-Hungarian Empire had a standing army of around 3 million soldiers and the Ottoman Empire had a regular army of 150,000 men in 1914.

Whatever the size of the armies at the outbreak of war in August 1914, the mobilisation that followed over the next four years, and the rate of casualties, are astonishing. We risk drowning in numbers – but what a horror story they tell. Over 5.1 million men dead on 'our side', with 12.8 million wounded. Around 3.4 million men perished on the 'other side', with over 8.4 million wounded. Over 42.1 million men had been mobilised to fight on 'our side' in this Great War, with around fifty-two per cent becoming 'casualties'. On the 'other side', around 22.85 million had been mobilised, with an even higher 'casualty' rate at over sixty-seven per cent (see the online Encyclopaedia Britannica section on World War One).

So many uniforms were made for the participants in this Great War.

So much blood was absorbed into their ruined fabric after the metal hit.

So many of the bodies these uniforms were covering ceased to breathe.

And for what?

When the so-called peace makers, the political elites of the victorious nations, met at the Versailles conference after the war ended, the peace terms they imposed on Germany were ruthless. The leaders of what was now the Weimar Republic following the abdication of Kaiser Wilhelm II, were compelled to acknowledge Germany's responsibility for the start of the war by signing a war-guilt clause. They also had to confirm the loss of the German Empire and agree to the payment of crippling reparations to the victorious Allied Powers. Through such short-sightedness, the seeds were sown for the emergence in Germany of the Nazi Party, which promised a revival of pride in the Fatherland. Thus began a sequence of events that led to another Great War, fought between 1939 and 1945, and featuring many of the same participant nations. More young men from across the world were once again fighting – and many dying – for their country.

What do the sources above tell of how a nation fights a war? Foremost, there is the division of the nation into recruiting areas. Lord Kitchener was not only responsible for the fighting of the war on the battlefield but also, through the War Office, recruitment. His potential soldiery were young men who had been primed in their local board schools – there had been primary education for all since the 1870s – to accept that it was their duty to be prepared to die for sovereign and country. Willingness to fight and kill, and perhaps die, was a conditioned response, for some at least. And it did not disappear. I remember winning the school's Junior Elocution Prize in 1961, reciting this verse from a tuneful hymn, no.319, in *Songs of Praise*:

I vow to thee, my country, all earthly things above,
Entire and whole and perfect, the service of my love;
The love that asks no questions, the love that stands the test,
That lays upon the altar the dearest and the best; the love that never falters, the love that pays the price,
The love that makes undaunted the final sacrifice.

These words were taken from verses written by Sir Cecil Spring Rice (1859-1918), a British diplomat who had served as the British ambassador to the USA from 1912-1917 and helped persuade the American president, Woodrow Wilson, to enter the war in 1917.

Cornish recruitment in 1914 had been assigned by the War Office to Lady Anne Warmington, the widow of the late first baron, Sir Cornelius Marshall Warmington (1842-1908), an English barrister and former Liberal MP who had died in 1908, six weeks after being given the new hereditary title. Within the corridors of power, she must have been regarded as a safe pair of hands. The Warmingtons may have been newcomers to the ranks of the wealthy and powerful, but Lady Anne performed her role with dexterity. Many of the masses would defer without question to the peerage. Remember the telling observation that a local made in 1982 about the annual pre-WWI Christmas Eve event at Tehidy for the widows of the miners who then applauded the generosity of Lord and

Lady Basset, ignoring the fact that their husbands had died young working to make the Bassets still richer (see above, p.44). Anne Warmington sought to persuade the women of Cornwall to join her as recruiters of their menfolk, making a 'special appeal' to use their 'influence' to persuade them 'to serve their king and country.'

Recruits to the Duke of Cornwall Light Infantry posed for the camera in 1915.[31]

Her plan included the razzmatazz – the 'processions with music', the 'patriotic concerts', the 'speeches... made to urge men to join Lord Kitchener's army.' Not, note, the British army, but 'Lord Kitchener's Army.' The men were being encouraged to see themselves as part of a quasi-feudal force, fighting for

---

31   Source: Bodmin Keep, Cornwall's Army Museum, who have given their kind permission for its use.

King, Country, and Empire. There was also a calculated effort to ensure that those recruited found themselves serving alongside those they knew from their own communities. Special 'Pals Battalions' were created across the country in the first two years of war before conscription was introduced in March 1916. They formed around twenty per cent of the 1,000 new battalions formed between 1914 and 1916.

Some men in Cornwall, however, found this clarion call to arms in the name of King, Country, and Empire particularly problematic. They were the members and attenders of the meeting houses of the Society of Friends, the Quakers, whose testimony impels them to peace and a rejection of war. Yet now they faced a clash. Did their duty to God trump their duty to king and country? During WWI, around thirty per cent of eligible Quaker men in the nation enlisted, choosing king and country; those who did not were split between 'absolutists', who refused any contact with the war, and those who were prepared to volunteer for ambulance and relief work overseas on the battlefields. Nationally, an estimated 16,000 men were registered as so-called 'conscientious objectors', 'Cos', from the 43,000 who had applied. Many of these Cos were Quakers. Within Cornwall, an online source cites sixty-two men as Cos, amongst whom was a remarkable Quaker, Wilfred Tregenza, from the parish of Paul where eighteen other men were also registered as conscientious objectors.

Wilfred Tregenza (1880-1974) was the son of a mayor of Penzance, educated at Truro College, who became the first Cornish boy to win a scholarship to Cambridge. Brought up as a Methodist, he became a teacher after graduating with a double first in mathematics. When war broke out, he registered as a conscientious objector, as did three of his brothers, warfare being contrary to the teachings of Jesus. He joined the Friends' Ambulance Unit (FAU) in France and served with distinction. When conscription was introduced in 1916, he heard that some Cos had been sentenced to be shot and was so moved that he returned to England to face conscription himself and seek registration as a CO. The tribunal treated him as a deserter and handed him over for a court martial, who sentenced him to ten years hard labour. Whilst he was in Dartmoor prison breaking stones for roadmaking, Tregenza was part of a group of Cos, escorted to a local church for a Sunday service, who were stoned by local villagers. Once the war was over, he was released from prison, joined the Quakers, resumed his teaching career, and ended up as a headmaster, inspector, and chair of the body that produced the Butler Education Report in 1944.

Another pacifist with a Cornish connection who found himself in trouble with both the local community and the authorities was the now celebrated writer, D.H. Lawrence (1885-1930). In the summer of 1916, Lawrence and his wife, the German-born Frieda, moved to Cornwall, settling in a remote cottage near the village of Zennor. They soon became the object of hostility and suspicion. Lawrence was known to be against the war; Frieda's name betrayed her German parentage. Their cottage was searched and trashed by the authorities after they were accused of spying and signalling to German submarines off the coast. In late 1917, the Lawrences were forced to leave Cornwall at three days' notice under the terms of the Defence of the Realm Act. The Cornish had no time for the writer from 'upcountry' who lacked a sense of duty – or worse.

Voluntary enlistment, spurred on by the likes of Lady Warmington, had provided the human material for a long war since August 1914, but demand began to outstrip supply. In January 1916, the Military Service Act was passed which meant all single men aged between eighteen and forty-one, with certain exceptions, became eligible for conscription. The impact on local communities must have been considerable; the death toll was already steadily mounting in the killing fields of battle and would continue to do so. On one single summer's day in 1916 on the Somme, the Sheffield City Battalion (12th York and Lancaster Regiment) lost 495 men, dead and wounded. In Cornwall, many men had joined the Duke of Cornwall's Light Infantry, which raised sixteen battalions and suffered 4,510 deaths during the war, although as the war years passed fewer and fewer Cornishmen were in the ranks of that regiment, as the story of Harry Patch has illustrated. Personal grief might have been tempered by notions of sacrifice in a good cause but the reality of a diminished family income for many would have been very hard.

The other focus for recruitment of Cornish men was, specifically, the tin miners. Their mining skills were now an instrument of war. By 1915, the Western Front had become a static line with a network of trench earthworks; these siege-like conditions led to a return to the siege-breaking technique of tunnelling and the recruitment of the military miner. In February 1915, eight Tunnelling Companies were formed as specialist units of the Corps of Royal Engineers; by mid-1916, the British Army had around 25,000 trained tunnellers, mostly volunteers taken from mining communities. The history of the Cornish miners of the 251 Tunnelling Company has been written by Robert Johns in *Battle Beneath the Trenches: The Cornish Miners of the 251 Tunnelling Company, RE* (2015). Johns explains that the mayor of Truro had been responsible for the formation of the 10th Battalion of the Duke of Cornwall's Light Infantry (Cornwall Pioneers) in March 1915, which was then referenced as the 'Cornish Miners battalion' in local newspapers. Most of these early recruits were then transferred to the Royal Engineers (RE) and formed the core of 251 Tunnelling Company in September 1915, with the names of 221 men recorded.

As Johns notes, the need for tunnellers came in response to the early success of German tunnellers in laying explosives in mines under Allied trenches. Recruitment of men such as Cornish miners who had the necessary experience and skills for working underground became vital, as is evident in their pay, which was far in excess of that of the infantry soldier. The tunnellers went on to a 'tunneller's mate' daily rate of 2s 6d, with their commanding officer in the field having the authority to bring them up to a daily rate of 6s, the 'skilled tunnellers' rate. An agreement between the Miner's Federation, which had been formed in 1888, and the War Office meant that fifty-seven per cent of miners would be classified as skilled tunnellers. The infantry soldier's daily basic pay was 1s.[32] According to Johns, such differences in pay were resented by many of the ordinary British 'Tommy' infantrymen, but they do help explain why so many Cornish men left local mines to volunteer for mining work beneath the fields of the Western Front on the continent of Europe,

---

32   2s 6d in 1916 = c.£12.50 today; 6s = c.£30 today; 1s = c.£5 today

both before conscription was introduced in 1916 and afterwards. Cornish miners were following the money; there were rich pickings to be had under those trenches with the daily payment so high – and casualties were lower than in the killing fields above.

Back in 1914, not all aristocratic ladies were as successful in their public presentation as Lady Anne Warmington. The letter referenced in the *Cornish Guardian* source suggests that Lady Maxwell should have known better than to accuse the men of the nation – 'England', by name – of 'cowardice and skulking' when the authorities claimed that insufficient numbers were volunteering. Her angry critic in London – G.A. Brittain – provides a perspective that has been largely overlooked: the cost to the family of war service. It seems from Brittain's figures that the volunteer's wife and any children would be left struggling to make household ends meet, given the 'paltry' allowance of 15s a week granted to the wife of a serviceman who also knew there was no death benefit payable on any life assurance.[33] The allowance had been substantially bigger a decade and a half earlier during the Boer War, but that was a small imperial war not the Great War. Those who held the nation's purse-strings seem to have decided that the country could not afford to be so generous since so many more men were needed to provide the 'human material for a long war.'

That same source, in early September 1914, acknowledges that Lord Kitchener may have to employ half-a-million more men if the nation is to win this war – something of an underestimate given the statistic that nearly 9 million men

---

33   15s in 1914 = c.£82 today

were mobilised within the British Empire during the war. Peace would come, it claimed, when 'We shall be, as we have been in the past, (the nation) most capable of continuing the war' – in other words, when the forces of the enemy were 'exhausted.' In fact, as noted above (p.140), 'our side' had 5.1 million dead; the Central Powers had lost 3.4 million men.

In the end, the factors that shaped the surrender of the Central Powers were their enforced commitment to a war on two fronts, in the West and in the East, from 1914 to 1917; the entry of the USA on the Allied side in 1917; and the political revolution in the autumn of 1918 in a German nation so weakened by five years of war.

Cornish scholarship has widened our understanding of the effects of this Great War on Cornwall. Sharron P. Schwartz and Roger Parker (1998), *Tin Mines and Miners of Lanner – The Heart of Cornish Tin*, provides a detailed account of these effects on a mining community in the parish of Lanner, about five miles west of Camborne. Their findings are indicative of a pattern that would have been similar in other villages and towns. Lanner had seen its largest mine – Tresavean – reopen in 1907 after years of economic slump. Then came the war in 1914. Parish records for 1915 show that Lanner had fifty-five men serving in the armed forces, nearly eight per cent of its adult male population. Eighty-six men eligible to fight remained but the Tresavean Mine experienced periodic stoppages throughout 1915 due to labour shortages. In October 1915, seventy-two men were recorded as having left the workforce, representing seventy-five per cent of the skilled labour force. By May 1916, the figure had risen to ninety-five men.

Not all, of course, survived. Sixteen Lanner men are

commemorated as among the war dead (see below, p.156). Of these, six were serving in the Duke of Cornwall's Light Infantry, five as privates and one as a 2nd lieutenant; and three were sappers in the Royal Engineers, 'tunnellers' under the trenches.

Unskilled labour was used to fill some of the labour shortage due to recruitment, and after conscription was introduced in 1916 the mine management got as many men as possible attested under statuary provisions to protect occupations 'of Cardinal Importance for the Maintenance of Trade and Industry'. The mine did continue to function until 1921, when it laid off its workforce as the global price of tin fell and the British government refused to take over the mine.

Tresavean Mine around 1910.[34]

The effects of the Great War on mining employment in Lanner was considerable – and similar effects were felt throughout Cornwall. Norikazu Kudo, in the online *KEIO Business Review* (No.50, 2015), provides a chronology of responses to the changing market conditions as they affected Cornish tin mining in the inter-war period from 1918-38. His data also

34   Source: www.imagearchive.royalcornwallmuseum.org.uk

shows that the number of men employed in tin mining in Cornwall fell from just over 7,000 in 1913, to around 5,800 in 1914, 5,000 in 1915, 4,800 in 1916, and around 4,600 in 1917. By the end of 1918, the figure for mining employment had recovered to around 5,300 men but then continued to decline steadily, before falling sharply and standing at around 500 men in 1922.

As for production of the tin ore, Cornish output fell steadily, if gently, from around 5,300 tons in 1913, to just over 5,000 in 1914, just under 5,000 in 1915, and then to 4,700 tons in 1916. Output then fell sharply in 1917 to around 3,800 tons, falling again to 3,200 tons in 1919 and 2,900 tons in 1920 before collapsing in the catastrophic years of 1921 and 1922. The shortage of skilled miners meant that development work to identify easily extractable ore deposits could not happen as before and so the average cost of mining rose.

Global factors had always played a part in shaping mining communities and they are again evident, as Norikazu Kudo suggests, in August 1918 when the price of tin soared to around £400 per ton. In response, the Allied Powers agreed to purchase strategic commodities, including tin, jointly, to distribute them effectively according to the needs of each country. The USA was rich in copper but poor in tin; the UK (that is, Cornwall) was rich in tin and by now poor in copper; adjustments were made accordingly, and the price of tin fell back. It seems likely that Cornish interests were set aside for the sake of ensuring that the American entry into the war was given as much British support as possible, including on this financial and economic front.

The effects of the Great War on Cornish communities are also evident in *The Cornishman* source, published shortly after the war had ended. It provides another reminder of the cost to the family, and the nation, of war service. Its report of the meeting of the Camborne and District War Pensions Committee in the previous week indicates the scale of the challenge facing a government committed to ensuring that 'every discharged man, and the dependents of serving men received all the benefits the Government intended they should have', especially when it had the additional responsibility of providing pensions to the dependents of those 'who had made the supreme sacrifice.'

A socialist revolution in Russia in 1917 served as a stark reminder to at least some of the wealthy and powerful in capitalist nations that a minimum of protection from hardship for the masses was advisable. There would have been local War Pensions Committees across Britain, following the guidelines laid down by the Ministry of Pensions and facing similar or heavier workloads to that in Camborne which had had thirty-six cases in that week alone. It had been early 1917 when the Ministry of Pensions had been set up in response to the failures in the existing system; it was an organization operating on an unprecedented scale. By the end of 1920, it had 19,121 staff and was overseeing the payment of 1,600,000 pensions at a cost of more than £23 million per year.[35]

The Great War had thus turned the government of Britain and its empire upside down in terms of its administration of benefits to family households in the motherland. Yet it was not only the administration of the country that had been radically changed. These five years of human loss and injury had a deeply traumatic effect, as the editorial in *The Cornish*

---

35 £23 million in 1920 = c.£1.2 billion today. For more information, see: https://www.westernfrontassociation.com/about-the-wfa/

Post and Mining News source written by Herbert Thomas suggests. Reflecting on the thirty years that had elapsed since he had returned from the USA and settled into a career in journalism, Thomas is drawn to the horror of the last five years which has left him amazed at the 'topsy-turveydom of things.' He concludes his piece by referring to the 'great crime of the war itself', which has cost 'at least ten million men in the pride of life.' [The total figure of war dead is now established as over 8.5 million; Thomas was not far from the mark.] He recognises the need for atonement and the necessity of starting 'all over again', in the hope that 'good will come out of evil.'

The war poet, Wilfred Owen (1893-1918), who was killed in action a week before the war ended, wrote in a poem of the 'old Lie': '*Dulce et decorum est pro patria mori*' – 'It is sweet and fitting to die for one's country.' Harry Patch broke through the self-imposed silence of nearly eighty years and wrote of his being 'thoroughly disillusioned', his religious faith 'shattered', by the time he was demobbed. Millions of young men across the world may have had, in varying degrees, similar feelings to those of Owen and Patch as the war dragged on and there were ever more casualties. Yet it did not lead to desertion or dereliction of duty in the case of most of the British forces. My sense is that the fighting men instinctively shut down to cope with the trauma and just continued obeying orders as they had been trained to do. After the war, most continued to numb their feelings in silence. The families left behind would have coped in similar ways, during and after the war. If the horrors of war were not enough, those who survived then had to face the trauma of the Spanish flu pandemic and the huge death toll from that viral invasion.

Herbert Thomas, now a middle-aged man in 1919, shows a degree of survivors' guilt as he suggests that: 'any middle-aged man, who saw a youth maimed or legless, ought to be ashamed that he is still alive and untouched by the war. I know that we middle-aged men ought to have stopped the bullets.'

Thomas also draws attention to the fact that the former ruler of the German Empire, Kaiser Wilhelm II (1859-1941) was now back to shooting game birds for recreation in exile in Holland, a fact which adds weight to my suggestion that there is a link between the slaughter of game birds and young men in battle. All the victims of war were, in a sense, under the control of the rich and powerful. Young men from Cornwall and across the world had been sucked into a vortex of nationalism and militarism beyond their ken. These matters had spun out of anyone's control for a time. It was not only working class men who became casualties in the Great War; their officers were also among the casualties of war and some of them were the sons of the wealthy and powerful. Geopolitical forces, shaped by the pursuit of profit from the control of land and resources and markets, had led to this global war between rival power blocs in which millions were killed and injured. The Cornish men who died [the Cornish Family History Society's most recent calculation is 6,419 men] had their lives cut short by a sweep of history they knew little about – in much the same way as the Cornish copper and tin mining industry had been shaped by global forces that were little understood and whose effects could be so devastating when the price of the ores fell, and mines closed. The ordinary miner's pursuit of a decent living was always at the mercy of economic forces beyond his control – and this at the same time as he faced the constant threat of death and injury at work due to his paymaster's unacknowledged greed.

The Cornish Family History Society has created a war website that is being constantly updated. A couple of decades ago, the members of the Society felt that details of those who had served and died for their country and had a connection with Cornwall should be collected in one dedicated website and, where possible, be accompanied by photographs of the individuals and the grave sites. Their volunteer members have found that of the 6,419 servicemen who perished, 5,440 were soldiers in the Army; 667 were sailors in the Royal Navy; 249 were sailors in the Royal Air Force. By a ratio of around 6:1, these Cornish men died in land battle rather than sea or air conflict.

The society also reported that these deaths included 224 sets of brothers; sixteen sets of fathers and sons; and there were twenty sets of fathers and sons where the father died in WWI and the son in WWII. Cornish women, left in charge of households and usually children, were the recipients of the proverbial 'bad news'. There would have been so much lamentation in Cornish towns and villages.

And the tears were only paused for a couple of decades. When the fatality figures for the two World Wars are compared, the figure for Cornish service personnel deaths in WWII is lower than in WWI – 4,786 compared with that breathtaking figure of 6,419 – but still remarkably high. This time, in WWII, there is a more even spread of death between the Services with 2,692 soldiers, 847 Royal Navy sailors, 232 Merchant Navy sailors, and 1,359 Royal Air Force members identified as fatalities in this second Great War. Fifty-four sets of Cornish brothers died in WWII, compared with the

224 in WWI, suggesting perhaps that both the pattern of recruitment was not quite the same and that the number of children in Cornish families had declined between the Great Wars.

The intention of the Cornish Family History Society is to honour the name of all the Cornish who have served in the armed forces and died in war. They have done a remarkable job. Based on their research, Cornwall Live – an online commercial media website – is able to present an interactive map of every village and town in Cornwall, which contains the figures of all those from each location who perished in the Great War, together with their name, rank and date of death.[36]

Selecting only some of these locations, here are the totals of the war dead in a range of towns and villages, moving from north to south in the part of Cornwall which features in this book:

Illogan – 71
St Day – 38
Redruth – 140
Tuckingmill – 58
Camborne – 90
Lanner – 16
Penponds – 34
Phillack – 26
Hayle – 15
St Erth – 16
St Ives – 79
St Just – 48

---

36 See: https://www.cornwalllive.com/news/history/remember-ing-cornwall-first-world-war-2205296

These were appalling, unprecedented losses. Cornish communities had been ripped apart – and linked to that devastation is the evidence of a need to commemorate. War memorials and church-stained glass and wall inscriptions became the means to memorialise those who had died.

Camborne Parish Church, and the war memorial still covered in poppies after the November 2022 Remembrance Day service. (17.01.23)

One can speculate on the psychology that explains this commitment to record, after a war, those who had lost their lives in the service of King and Country.

Was it a gesture to show that these lives had not been wasted? These men would now live on through the carving of their names on surfaces of stone or glass; their service would be honoured and stand as an inspiration to other generations.

Camborne war memorial remains a site of remembrance for communities in Camborne. (17.01.23)

Was it unacknowledged guilt? The rich and powerful were for the most part those too old to fight at the front; they would be absorbing most of the cost of these memorials; those slain were, for the most part, the masses of men at the bottom of the social pyramid of deference; in good conscience, were they not owed some small debt of recompense for having made the ultimate sacrifice?

Was it unconscious self-interest? These servicemen from the so-called lower orders, when they were not in military uniform, provided the labour that was necessary within the capitalist economy to produce the profits and serve the interests of those who could afford to employ such workers. Not to commemorate would be a social folly, an omission that would widen class divisions.

Was this new meme of memorialising the consequence of a new kind of Christian morality that had gathered momentum during the Victorian period? Many within the middle classes and the so-called upper-classes were now beginning to recognise that the teachings of Jesus did point to a less self-centred and more communitarian way of shaping society.

An inscription on the plinth of the Camborne war memorial; sentimental poetry that touches the horror of the Great War. The poppy wreaths shown are from the local Girls'Brigade and the Scout Group, and the Camborne Regeneration Group. (17.01.2023)

Alan Bennett, the Yorkshire dramatist, provides some background in *The History Boys* (2004) that shines a light on how recent this need was to memorialise. Hector, the school master, is explaining to Posner, the pupil, that Thomas Hardy in his poem 'Drummer Hodge' is writing about the Zulu Wars (1879) or possibly the Boer War (1899-1902):

> '...these were the first campaigns when soldiers... common soldiers... were commemorated, the names of the dead recorded and inscribed on war memorials. Before this, soldiers... private soldiers anyway, were all unknown soldiers, and so far from being revered there was a firm in the nineteenth century, in Yorkshire of course, which swept up their bones from the battlefields of Europe in order to grind them into fertiliser.
>
> 'So, thrown into a common grave though he may be, he is still Hodge the drummer. Lost boy though he is on the other side of the world, he still has a name.'

Hector may have been mistaken in linking the image of a war memorial with wars that preceded the Great War, but his general point holds. The common soldier has acquired a name in death. The war memorial is now such a common feature of so many British towns and villages that an understanding of the motives behind its creation after the first Great War and its reshaping after the second World War may be, for many, less than full. Death brings its own taboos, whether the dead man was a tin miner or a serviceman in uniform. Given these taboos, those still living had to find a way to come to terms with the finality of an event that awaits all of us and in their lifetime had taken from them so many in their society, through industrial disease and death, or through death in battle.

Stained glass memorial window in the Anglican parish church of St Just, recording the names of 38 of the 48 men in the St Just community who lost their lives fighting 'for King and Country' in the Great War, 1914-18. (02/03/23)

War memorials are in nearly every town and village in the land – here is the war memorial in St Just, photographed on a wet January day. (04.01.23)

My purpose, as the historian, has been to provide the background to such deaths. I have also sought to tease out the nature of an economic and social system that led to these premature deaths, through prioritising profit over the risk of injury and fatalities and waging war to advance the nation's share of the markets and resources in the world.

ANOTHER THIRTY-
ONE MINERS ARE KILLED
– THE LEVANT MINE
DISASTER ON
20 OCTOBER 2019

S ources:
The Cornish Post and Mining News – **Saturday 25
October 1919:**

LEVANT MINERS CRUSHED
COLLAPSE OF MAN-ENGINE IN SHAFT
THIRTY-ONE MEN KILLED

*The shock and sorrow following the news that three Levant
miners had been killed in the shaft on Monday, has been
changed to horror and dismay as the death toll has mounted
every day.*

*A certainty that twenty men have been crushed to death,
and that eleven missing men have probably shared their fate…*

makes it a more terrible event even than the Wheal Owles disaster, when in January 1893, twenty men were drowned by holing into a pool of water in a neighbouring mine.

The tragedy was the work of an instant. Something snapped – perhaps an iron cap or bolt – and what has been described as 'a living pillar of men', dropped down the man-engine shaft, crushing many to death, mangling more with debris of breaking wood and metal – the beam of the man-engine, the ladder ways in the side of the main shaft, and the platforms cut in the side of the shaft.

Imagine square wood beams 40 feet long, braced together in a long stem and held perpendicularly 1,800 feet in height in a mine shaft.

Jutting out of this beam, which moves up twelve feet and then down twelve feet, like the Cornish pump which raises the water and drains the mine, are steps. On each step stands a man, and from 130 to 150 were standing as a human pillar on this structure or waiting on the side platforms to take the next step, as they ascended from their work. About twelve had stepped off in safety on reaching the surface.

The men having completed their day's work about 2.30 pm, the machine was practically full of men, each one, as it were, standing above the head of the other on the projecting step.

An instant later all these men would have stepped off and paused on the side platforms, or sollars, for the next uplift of the engine. That instant meant life or death to thirty or more men.

The scenes were indescribable. The rod, released from its top, cracked in several places, and the structure crashed down in a mass of debris...

The man-engine at the Dolcoath Mine, Camborne, photographed by J.C. Burrows at 234 fathoms in 1893. Miners can be seen standing on the steps of the engine rod while others stand on solars at the side.[37]

The Cornish Post and Mining News – Saturday 25 October 1919:

Levant is one of the oldest working mines in the county, and it was the last to use the man-engine, which has been regularly inspected and the materials renewed at various times. It is also the last of the mines worked on the cost-book, or unlimited liability system [Unlimited liability meant that the individuals who owned the mine were liable for the company's debts; being 'worked on the cost-book' meant that the company's capital, its wealth, was only what was recorded in the accounts as the profit left after subtracting the expenditures from the income from sales. See below,

37   Source: www.imagearchive.royalcornwallmuseum.org.uk

pages 179, for details of the switch to limited liability in the aftermath of the disaster.]

Levant is perched on the edge of cliffs, and its tin and copper are raised from a mile and more under the bed of the Atlantic.

LEVANT MINE, ST. JUST.
THE SCENE OF THE RECENT DISASTER.

Levant Mine[38]

It was managed for many years by the late Major Robert White up to the time of his death; and the late Mr. Francis Oats was the chairman, Major Francis Freethy Oats succeeding his father. Committee members include Mr. T. Robins Bolitho, Mr. J.C. Tregarthen, Mr. Henry Olds, and Mr. Harry Rowe of Camborne.

…The mine was on the brink of being reconstructed – and a new vertical shaft, with gig for lowering and raising men, formed part of the scheme.

38　Source: *The Cornish Post and Mining News* – Saturday 25 October 1919 – p.5

The Cornishman and Cornish Telegraph – Wednesday 29 October 1919:

Lucky Escape

Our representative had an interview with Mr. John Grenfell, son of John Edward Grenfell, one of the shift bosses who unfortunately was killed. Mr. Grenfell himself was amongst those who had stepped off the man-engine before the accident happened. He also said that all the boys had been saved in this manner and explained technically why this should have been so. He considers that between 40 and 50 escaped thus, and therefore, about 100 men would have been left on the man-engine when the irons snapped. Mr. Grenfell said that two steps beneath him on the man-engine was Mr. Howard Carbis, who perceiving the sudden descent, leaped for the level, which he succeeded in reaching and thus saved his life…

It is stated that no men who were below the 140 fathom level were killed.

A Plucky Miner

One who was present at the interview and was in possession of the facts said that "Mr. Grenfell was the first man to go down to the assistance of his colleagues".

"No", replied Mr. Grenfell, with most becoming modesty, "If you put in anything, say that William Oats and John Grenfell were the first two who went down after the accident, from the surface."

"There were many others by to help", added Mr. Grenfell, "and we were able to send up Thomas Maddern. After that the rope was again sent down and I was lowered another 36 ft. A lot of debris came down around me, but here I found Jos. Hosking, who was shouting out for light and assistance.

"When he had been sent up I found I could not do anything more for those below, owing to the chokage in the shaft; even though I could hear someone groaning."

This must undoubtedly have been Nicholas Hocking Thomas, who was rescued under such dramatic conditions on Wednesday night… The work that night was difficult and dangerous – dangerous not only to those who were conducting the operation, but also to the man himself unless due precautions were taken to prevent the debris from falling away.

The volunteer party from East Pool (Camborne) were among those who were conducting this work, and the fact that groans could be heard from the man as late as two o'clock on Wednesday afternoon spurred them on in their efforts. From that moment, however no sound was heard proceeding from him. But the work never relaxed, and at about 8.30 on Wednesday night, they found him near the adit, in a standing position on the "sollar" as the platform at the side of the shaft is called. Dr. Richmond was in attendance but the poor fellow breathed his last before he could be taken to the dry [**the miners' washing and changing area**].

A Marvellous Escape

A graphic description of the accident, and its terrible consequences was supplied by Robert Penaluna, a young St Just miner who was on the man-engine at the time of the breakage.

"I was coming up on the man-engine", he said, "three steps below the 150 fathom level. The engine was full of men. We had travelled up part of the way between one sollar and another when the engine dropped a little but then picked herself up again. Then she fell away to the bottom. I was thrown on my chest upon the sollar. My chum on the next sollar below

(Charlie Freestone, aged 25, of St Just) had his feet caught between the step on which he stood and the sollar, and was swung upside down."

"I was not hurt except that a piece of timber struck me on the leg. For about three hours I was down there before I could come up. Then I walked up the ladder through the pumping engine shaft, to the surface. Before that I picked up Charlie Freestone, who was suffering from shock, and dragged him through a manhole on to the sollar upon which I was standing. He fainted in my arms. We got him back to the 150 level shaft and men of the afternoon shift helped to drag Freestone to the surface with ropes.

"When the engine broke it was a tremendous crash for in dropping she knocked away timber and everything in her path. The engine rod on which we were travelling shook violently. The smash gave a terrible shock to us all, and everybody lost heart and nerve entirely. The screams of some of the men were awful, as they gripped the rod like grim death. A number of them had the presence of mind to jump to the nearest place, and saved themselves by the skin of their teeth."

"I wouldn't go through an experience like that again for the world."

Boy's Terrible Experience

William Lawry, a bright young lad, and son of Mr. Richard Lawry of Queen Street, St Just, who started work underground only about three weeks ago had a very narrow escape. He was fortunate in escaping serious injury, but he was suffering from shock when taken home in the Penzance ambulance car. In describing his experience he said one man lay across him dead, and the body had to be removed before he could be rescued.

The Last Body Recovered

The body of the last of the victims, Edwin Trathen, was discovered on Saturday morning and brought to the surface from the 80 fathom level. The deceased was superintendent of Bojewyan Sunday School and organist. He was also a Class leader. Within about twelve months no fewer than four funerals have left Mr. Trathen's home, his wife having died about a year ago.

BBC – *Yesterday's Witness* – 1970:

In 1969, the BBC made a film in the *Yesterday's Witness* series to mark the fiftieth anniversary of the Levant mine disaster. It was produced and directed by Stephen Peet. Now available on YouTube, thanks to the Association for Cornish Heritage, this documentary provides a remarkable opportunity to see and hear miners and family who lived through this day and the aftermath. Their testimony provides a layer of historical evidence which includes material that was not reported in the media or official reports fifty years before. John Corin, edited and expanded by Peter Joseph (2013), *Levant – A Champion Cornish Mine*, has included quotes from what Corin calls 'some of the more dramatic passages' and I have used these below, as well as my transcripts of other interviews in which the dialogue records unreported concerns about the man-engine.

The YouTube presentation is a compilation of the BBC film (around 30 minutes) from 1969, and extracts from interviews in 1979 with Ted Gundry, one of the founders of Radio Cornwall, who is narrating in 1979 and again in 1982 (around 17 minutes).

Testimony from *Yesterday's Witness*:

Lionel Ellis (surface driver for the man-engine from 1912 to 1917) – 'It was a lovely engine house, really – 180 feet from here to there – I was just an engine driver, that's all. By 1917, I'd got frightened. The manager was a sick man and I went to the chief engineer and said I am not working on this anymore. You put me on another engine or I'm shifting from here altogether. He got me a job on another engine a few miles further up. Two weeks later, came the accident. [Lionel Ellis must have been waiting to start on the new engine; on the day of the 'accident' he was still at Levant but not on that fatal morning shift – see below, p.174.]

William Lawry (the 'bright young lad' from the newspaper source above who had started work in 1919, aged fourteen) – 'In this district there were four male voice choirs and most of the men worked in the mines – the sound that came out of the shaft as the miners travelled that man-engine was out of this world. [Another miner, unidentified, added later]: 'There were men who didn't believe in church or chapel and that sort of thing but everyone joined in the hymns...'

William Lawry (speaking later in the interview) – 'I was two steps above what we call the 80, that's eighty fathoms [480 feet below surface], when the engine broke away and I was dug out two steps below that – a matter of 48 feet. Now the man that I worked with, he was a step above me and he was found down 110 [660 feet below surface], and the man that was below me, a man called Willie Walters, he was dug out before they found me, and he was dead. So actually I was very, very fortunate. I had 36 stitches in my face and neck, lost all my front teeth, a collar broke, and eight ribs crushed.

But – took me 12 months before I started to work again.' (See John Corin (2013), p.45).

Harold Semmens, with his wife (Levant miner who survived the disaster; his brother, Leonard Semmens, who had only recently returned as a survivor from the Great War, was one of the thirty-one victims) – 'All of us were nervous. Numbers left. We all feared something would happen. There were lots of creaking noises. I stayed on but my wife's brother left because he was afraid of the man-engine. He knew something would happen.

'One day, after the disaster, my mother saw the manager and mine captain approaching in the street and she went out and called them everything under the sun – murderers, and everything.'

Mrs. Semmens – 'Thanks to you, she said, you've murdered my son. You've murdered my boy.'

Harold Semmens – 'And from then on, I got marked. I couldn't get a job there.'

Anita Murley (wife of William Murley, who died in the disaster; she was 27 and seven months pregnant with their third child, he was 29) – 'I heard them talking a few weeks before the accident – my husband and two other underground friends – and they were discussing about the man-engine then and I heard them saying that it was making a lot of creaking noise which they didn't like – so they thought it should have been seen into – but I don't think it ever was - because if they had tried something, it wouldn't have happened – and then it did happen and it cost all those men's lives.

'He got up at 6 that morning and I got him a cooked breakfast and prepared his lunch for him and I saw him off to work at 6.30. He came running back after five minutes – he had forgotten his match box. Some say that was a bad omen…

'They always said that the engineer was supposed to inspect the man-engine every morning but I think they were working the mine as hard as they could to get the most out of it for themselves – the managers and others - things were very neglected…

'We got so much every fortnight at first but it was eleven months before we got any compensation. The MP for Plymouth got it for us, he fought for us – it didn't seem as if the mine intended to pay it – they didn't want to.

'When my children were growing, money was very short - they needed more food and boots and clothes – they gave us what they called 'a living' but it was not enough - so I went out washing two days a week – when I asked for money for their boots, they said I needed to be rearing my children. There were thousands in that fund which should have been spent and it never was.'

Albert Dymond (Levant miner, not on the morning shift) – 'And I had a mate, he was there for a day and half to two days and when he came out – seen 'un day or two afterwards. 'Well, what was it like, boy?' 'Well', he said, 'it was like 'ell – a mass of fire with the iron and the wood and the stones all comin' down – a mass of fire.' [The 'mass of fire' referred to here is, of course, an image from the reality of being under enemy fire in the Great War – it took me a while to appreciate this allusion.] An' he was there for a day, day and a half standin' on this 2ft platform or step holdin' on to that. No light. He could'n move 'cause he didn't know whether he'd go down farther or not. He was there 'till someone fetched him out.' (See John Corin (2013), pp.44-45).

Albert Dymond (speaking later in the interview) – 'I said to Lionel Ellis (the surface engine driver, quoted above) when the Inquiry started, "Why aren't you going?" He said, "I haven't been invited. They know if I go, I will tell the truth."'

Lionel Ellis (Engine driver) – 'I wasn't on the shift that day. The man who was on the engine that Monday wanted to keep his job. He went and told them what he was told to say. Yes – he sold his own soul to keep his job on the mine.'

John James (Levant miner, not on the morning shift) – 'We were stretcher bearers, you know, has to take 'em back, found two down where I was doing in 50 level, one down and one up on the next stage. We brought they two back, in there 'bout hour and half we was, then we got from there up 60 level, went up there and brought three or four back, dead. Then we's sent from there up 24 level and I think I, without tellin' a lie, I think we carried twelve back from there that night. I was afternoon shift. I went down 2 o'clock and never went home no more till 8 o'clock next evenin' and 'bout twelve we carried out there and two of them was our neighbours here. Yes, funerals here, funerals there, for days and days and days.' (See John Corin, 2013, pp.47-48).

Ted Gundry interview extracts – from 1979:

Mrs. Anita Nokes (daughter-in-law of the Manager of Levant in 1919, Captain Ben Nicholas, who was also one of its shareholders) – 'One of the things that has never been mentioned as far as I know is the fact that my father-in-law did help the wives and families of the victims entirely out of his own pocket and the kindness of his heart. Even though he was not involved in any way, he was the kind of man who would have helped anyone who needed help and did so a number of occasions, not only at Levant.'

Ted Gundry – 'Whilst everything was done to alleviate the hardship, [There is an inconsistency here: Gundry had earlier explained that a disaster fund was started but took some time to administer] nothing could have been done to replace the loved ones lost in the disaster. So should the disaster have happened in the first place?'

Levant miner, unidentified – 'Anyone who understands timber work knows that the timber was absolutely rotten – yet it was supposed to hold that heavy man-engine shaft – it was incapable of doing the job it was put there to do – and I'm fairly certain that the management must have known about it and put off the end day because of the expense and what have you – it just wasn't done and it should have been done – in my opinion.'

Ted Gundry narrating in 1982 – 'Immediately afterwards a fund was started, donations coming from all quarters including Cornish miners abroad in South Africa, America, and Australia. Payments were made as soon as possible, but no record of the amounts still exist. However, in January 1921, the charity commissioners appointed trustees for a scheme to manage the funds then totalling £28,000. This was invested and the interest provided the working capital which up to 1979 totalled £70,000, paid to the 34 dependents over the years the fund had been administered. In 1979, there was still £20,000 in the bank. On the 60th anniversary of the disaster in 1979, Mrs. Anita Murley was the only surviving dependent. She had had three children to support and, in addition, she had had to assist her husband's mother who didn't receive any assistance from the fund at all – just 7s 6d from the Parish.[39] In the past, the people of St Just have been critical of the way the trustees had handled these funds in those early days, as Anita Murley told me in 1979':

Mrs. Anita Murley – [Now affectionately known in the district as 'Granny Murley', aged 87 in 1979] – 'If you had a good month for pay [down the mine], you might get two months when he would hardly get anything. They hadn't got enough to pay for the candles and the dynamite that they had to pay for themselves.

'The money [from the Disaster Fund] could have been circulated among us better. When you've got little growing children you always want boots and different things – and there was always quite a bit of scheming to work out how to pay for them. I went through it and I know.'

Ted Gundry – 'So should the original trustees have been a little more generous when the need was greater? It was a point I put to Major Simon Bolitho in 1979 when he was chairman of the Levant disaster fund.'

Major Bolitho – 'I think looking at the position from today's point of view that is probably so. The trustees at the time apparently felt it was their duty to relieve real need – the need had to be shown – and then money was paid out. But no money was paid out for anything in the way of comforts or luxuries.'

Ted Gundry – 'There was no memorial plaque to mark the disaster and several people I spoke to thought there should be some kind of recognition. So I put this to Major Bolitho who thought it was an excellent idea and assured me he would raise the matter at the next trustee's meeting. Three

39 £28,000 in 1921 = c.£1.75 million today; £20,000 in 1979 = c.£130,000 today; 7s 6d in 1921 = c.£23.50 today

years later, in 1982, a memorial plaque was unveiled at the Trewellard Methodist chapel at the top of Levant Road, quite close to the Levant site. Lord Falmouth, the Lord Lieutenant of Cornwall [the official representative of the Crown] presided. Mrs. Anita Morley, the sole surviving widow, was also there.'

Mrs. Anita Murley [now aged 90; she passed away in 1985, three years later] – 'I thought the service was lovely – really I did – mind you, I was all of a shake – it brings it home to you – but I'm very pleased it's taken place.' [A few years later, decline in attendance led to the closure of Trewellard Chapel and the removal of the memorial tablet to Geevor Mine - finally shut as a mine in 1990 and now open to visitors.]

The man-engine was installed at the Levant mine in 1857 when there were around 800 men, boys, and girls recorded as working for the mining company. It was hailed as a splendid advance since it eliminated the fatigue and dangers experienced by miners who had previously walked up and down ladders to reach the bottom of the shaft. Miners received no pay for the time it took them to reach their lodes, and then return after their shift. It took one hour to descend by ladder; to ascend, it took one hour and a half. There was the ever-present risk of slipping and plunging to an even earlier grave. There was also the time taken to walk through the tunnel to reach the lode over a mile out under the sea. So, for miners, the half-hour journey using the man-engine was very much a blessing.

However, not all was good news. The mine management displayed a lack of concern for safety that attracted the attention of the government inspectorate when the man-engine was extended in 1888 by 266 feet to reach a depth of 1600 feet; John Corin (2013) notes that 'no knocker or signalling line was provided' at that time and the Inspector of Mines saw to it that two members of the committee, who were large shareholders, were sued. Corin also reports that in 1908 there was an incident when a length of the rod broke and several men were injured, some severely – 'and it was with considerable difficulty that the severely injured men were brought to the surface... but the management seems to have been little roused by the incident.'

There were basic safety devices fitted to the man-engine and these seem to have worked in that 1908 incident. The rod had wings, or catch-pieces, with corresponding sills, stout pitch pine beams, fixed in the mine shaft. It was these safety devices which failed eleven years after that first broken rod incident when, on 20 October 1919, the rod again parted from the beam at the surface. Corin explains that the rod, in falling, got out of line, missing the upper sills and catches and destroying others, and broke in two at sixty fathoms. The upper part, with thirty men on it, then fell sixty feet to the seventy fathom level, destroying platforms as it went. This fall caused most of the casualties.

By the time of this disaster in 1919, the man-engine had become a virtual museum piece, the only one left still working in Cornwall. The testimony of members of the mining community, such as Lionel Ellis, Mr. and Mrs. Harold Semmens, and Anita Murley, recorded in the BBC documentary *Yesterday's Witness* in 1969 shows that many of those who trusted their lives to this ancient man-engine did so nervously. Some refused to take the risk and left the mine. This was a tragedy waiting to happen, in the absence of action from the mine management.

However, the men in that management closed their minds to the immediate problems. There seems to have been a recognition that the mine needed reconstruction – the *Cornish Post and Mining News* in 1919 reported that the company was on the brink of implementing such a plan. That same source also sets out the management position that the man-engine was regularly inspected and fit for purpose. But the reality was very different. The Levant mining company was hard-pressed for funds. It was now the only surviving cost-book mining company in Cornwall and had no reserves under its antiquated system of bookkeeping. Capitalism required efficient, more modern ways of accumulating capital and the system at the Levant mine was not up to scratch. Thirty-one men lost their lives as a consequence.

Within three months of the disaster, just before Christmas 1919, an agreement was reached with the Geevor mining company to form a new limited company, Levant Tin Mines Ltd, to take over the working of Levant, with an authorised capital of £160,000 in 320,000 shares, each one costing 10s.[40] The capital thus raised allowed the mine to stagger on 'against all the odds and its manifest deficiencies', in John Corin's words, for a few more years. But the absence of such capital before the disaster helps explain why that tragedy happened.

Another factor that needs to be taken into account is the worsening relationship between management and

---

40   £160,000 in 1919 = c.£10.6 million today; 10s in 1919 = c.£33 today

miners. Corin outlines a period of industrial dispute between 1917 and 1919. In February 1918, the mining company had refused the union's demands for an increase in wages and a minimum wage rate, despite the shortage of labour which would normally have led to a rise in pay. The union was also pressing the Government for support for the tin mines of Cornwall at a time when the price of Cornish tin had been kept artificially low following the Anglo-American agreement of 1918 (see above, p.151) but none was forthcoming. A strike followed in the summer of 1918 during which feelings ran so high that the Chief Constable was asked to provide police protection for those men who wished to continue to work. The death in that year of Captain Frank Oats, who had a quarter share in the ownership of the Levant mine, led to his son, Colonel Francis Freathy Oats, taking over and threatening to close the mine. That threat brought a temporary settlement of the dispute, but the summer of 1919 brought more industrial conflict, with another rejected wage demand followed by another threat to close the mine.

There is no word of these strikes or industrial disputes in the oral testimony of those who lived through these years and were still alive in the 1960s, 1970s and 1980s when they were recorded on film. There is, however, as we have seen above, compelling evidence that there were many in the mining community who knew that the man-engine was no longer safe and also felt they could do nothing to persuade management to act on that knowledge. Lionel Ellis knew that he was seen as 'just an engine driver'; he also reported that the manager was 'a sick man.'

Yet none of this emerged in the official inquiry's report,

delivered to the Home Department in London in December 1919, and shared in the Cornish local press in these words:

> 'The coroner summed up the evidence, saying he did not think that there had been any culpable neglect... The jury having retired, returned the following verdict: Death was accidental, the cause being due to fatigue of a defective part of the metal.'

Corin observes that 'such a disaster would no doubt bring more legal consequences today' but he still reports that:

> 'The whole subject was very thoroughly examined in great detail. The conclusion of the cause of the failure of the engine was very simple. The rod was attached to the beam at the top by two strap plates, in the shape of an elongated U. It had been annealed three years before, but a close inspection when it was hot had failed to reveal a flaw in its manufacture which led to its eventual breakage.'

I have made the argument already, with regard to the Wheal Owles disaster (see above, pp.84-86), that those with a vested interest can manipulate science to attempt to blind others to the truth. There is a case to be made here, with respect to the Levant disaster, that not only could this tragedy have been avoided, but the official verdict may have been shaped by a misrepresentation of the scientific evidence available. There was enough sense within the mining community of a tragedy waiting to happen to justify a much more critical examination of the circumstances of this disaster. But the conclusions of a more rigorous inquiry may well have damaged the interests of those with power and wealth – and that reluctance to probe deeper still lingers, even in John Corin's treatment of the issue. He acknowledges that he was 'tempted to include the whole transcript as an appendix' but then states that 'quotes from some of the more dramatic passages must suffice' (p.44). I have provided, in the sources above, my transcripts of those interviews in *Yesterday's Witness* in which substantial evidence emerges to suggest that management failed to address the justified concerns of some of their miners.

Nevertheless, as the sources above show, the newspaper accounts of the disaster at the time do accept the official line that this was a tragic accident. Sixty-three years later, in 1982, that line was still being carefully followed when the memorial plaque was unveiled in the Trewellard chapel. The Ted Gundry source material includes a sequence in which the minister presiding at the memorial service makes an explicit reference to the 'accident' in which thirty-one miners lost their lives. 'It was', he said, the 'price they paid for winning tin.'

Indeed.

The manager of Levant had been seen by Lionel Ellis as a sick man. Further research identified him as Captain Ben Nicholas and also revealed evidence of the tensions between workers in the Levant mining community and this manager after the disaster. I have referenced Raymond Williams' notion of a 'structure of feeling' already and suggested that at any time there is likely to be more than one such structure of feeling evident in a community. There were, therefore, different ways of seeing Captain Ben Nicholas. His daughter-in-law, speaking in 1979, had presented an almost saintly picture; others, such as the mother of one of the victims of the disaster, Leonard Semmens, had a very different image. She accused Captain Nicholas of murdering her son.

An online site for a local history group in St Just and Pendeen has been the source for further detail about Captain Ben Nicholas (1871-1926).[41]

A member of the Institute of Mining Engineers, he had worked in South Africa, Brazil, and, closer to home, as an agent at the Dolcoath mine. He was also a freemason who rose to be a Mark Master Mason of the Mount Edgcumbe Lodge in Camborne; he had served as chairman of the St Just Urban Council and sat as a magistrate on the West Penwith Bench. Captain Nicholas had also been a trustee at Trewellard, Bojewyan and Morvah Wesleyan chapels. This was a man of considerable social standing.

He took over the management of the Levant Mine in 1907 at the age of thirty-six years, remaining there until his retirement shortly before his death, nineteen years later. His grand-daughter – Pam Urquhart – who now lives in Canada records that:

'He and my grandmother were mainly involved with Bojewyan chapel but Capt. Ben left there at some point when he was mine manager due to the fact that the miners were treating him very badly – this was the time when the unions were getting started and some union officials came to Levant and got the miners up in arms about their low pay which they took out on

---

41 See: https://www.suejames.org/st-just-and-pendeen-memories/ttps

Capt. Ben. He feared for his life so carried a gun and had a bodyguard.

'He was quite upset about this as although their pay was low, he was very good to them in terms of giving them eggs, butter, firewood, etc from the farm and generally looking out for those in real need. The miners were all Methodists and Capt. Ben was very hurt by the fact that they were very unappreciative of all that he did for them – he therefore left Bojewyan chapel and went to Pendeen church, while my grandmother continued to go to Bojewyan.'

A critical divide is evident. Captain Ben Nicholas and his family had their way of seeing the world; the mining community's way of seeing matters was very different. Harold Semmens knew that he had been unable to get a job at Levant after his mother, in her grief, had lost control and told Captain Nicholas to his face that he was a murderer. If deference was not shown, there was a price to pay. Any common thread of Methodist religious belief was not enough to bridge this gap, such was the strength of feeling on both sides.

For historians shaped by the insights of Karl Marx, the sources in this section point to a class divide with the poor, exploited miners and their families in one camp and on the other side, there is a privileged elite whose wealth has been generated by the labour of those miners. This elite controls and shapes so much of that mining community's living and dying yet fails to understand why such a community is not more grateful. Outsiders, such as the union [the Dockers' Union were representing the interests of the Levant miners in 1919], are targeted for blame; paranoia is apparent in the reported anxiety that Captain Nicholas felt for his own security; there is a clear determination to maintain the right to decide what is a 'real need', without an empathic consultation with the intended beneficiaries.

That same assumed right to determine a 'real need' is also apparent in the work of the trustees of the Levant Disaster Fund who administered that charity during its lifetime. Their definition of such a need was responsible for keeping the dependents of the victims impoverished, as the testimony of Mrs Anita Murley illustrates. When the moneys from the Disaster Fund were distributed, it was according to supposed need, so a means-test was applied. Those already in receipt of a pension, for example, had that pension sum deducted from the compensation payment. Somehow William Lawry, who had been fourteen when he survived the disaster and too young to qualify for state aid, got nothing from the fund. His father was too proud to ask for relief.

Throughout this book, I have been tracing a separation of interests between the wealthy elite and those beneath them 'in a social hierarchy that had been ordained by those who had held power over generations' (see above, p.6 and following). I have demonstrated that in a capitalist industrialising society where profit is more valued than people, the unregulated pursuit of greater personal wealth will come at the expense of the health and even life of those at the bottom of this hierarchy (see above, pp.16-18). The Levant Mine disaster of 1919 and its aftermath bears a terrible witness to these truths.

Remains of the Man-Engine shaft at the Levant Mine, the scene of the 1919 disaster which cost the lives of 31 miners – I took this photograph in April 2022 during a visit guided by John Toman, my Cornish friend to whom this book is dedicated.

THE END-TIME FOR CORNISH TIN MINING

Sources:
Cornubian and Redruth Times – **Thursday 25 August 1921:**

LOCAL UNEMPLOYMENT
Touching letter to the Prime Minister
SITUATION "ACUTE, DISTRESSFUL AND DEPLORABLE."
Request for an interview

The Mining Division Unemployment Committee met at Camborne on Friday evening, Mr. F.J. Lee presiding. At the previous meeting a small committee was appointed to consider means of approaching the Prime Minister in order to put before him the serious position in their area, also to ask for special consideration for the out of work miners. At Friday's meeting it was reported that the following letter had been sent to Mr. Lloyd George:

"In accordance with urgent instructions from a large and important meeting of representatives of public bodies and others

interested in the tin mining of Cornwall, we write to solicit the favour of an interview to submit for your serious consideration the acutely distressful and desperate conditions of almost the entire locality connected with the tin mining industry... we will prove that the position of the Cornish miners is peculiarly exceptional and that they are entitled to special consideration and treatment."

The letter was signed by the chairmen of Redruth and Camborne Urban, Redruth Rural and St Just Urban Councils, the Joint Industrial Council for the Redruth Board of Guardians, the secretary of the Industrial Council, and the secretary of the Unemployment Committee. No reply has yet been received from Mr. Lloyd George.

...Mr. F.F. Oats, of St Just, wrote: "I note that the Joint Industrial Council has nominated me amongst others, but I much regret that I have not the time to act, nor am I in sympathy with any government subsidies for any industries as I am positively certain that the interference of the government in any subsidies simply means the squandering of public money and impossible conditions of working."

The Secretary (Rev. W.A. Bryant) thought Mr. Oats had misunderstood the position, for they were not applying for a subsidy.

It was decided to point this out to Mr. Oats.

[...]

Mr. Henry Grylls declared, from the floor: "the miners and their families will be very greatly in want before long. Is this a matter which is going to be dealt with by this committee by voluntary subscription, or is it to be left to the Poor Law authorities to be dealt with through the rates?... I know there are a number of people who consider the latter way of dealing with the difficulty is the better. I am not one of these – (hear, hear), – not because I have any desire to prevent the matter coming to the rate-payers – the rate-payer has no sympathy from me in this matter at all – but for the sake of the women and children we are trying to help, it will be a great pity if we cannot carry on and help them by voluntary means. As we are going on from fortnight to fortnight, it seems a little hopeless, and I am uncomfortable about our financial position as reported by the Treasurer. I hope the committee will consider something to help the funds. To my mind a personal appeal is the best means, as I have urged before."

[The newspaper article then continued with an editorial commentary in which the hand of Herbert Thomas (see above, pp.130-131) is evident]

It must not be forgotten – and this is a point which no doubt will be especially pressed on the Prime Minister should he grant the desired interview before his departure for the continent on his holiday – that the closing of the Cornish mines is largely the sequel to the patriotic efforts they made to serve this country during the war, when the miners got no war wages comparable to those of the coal miners and the owners of the mines sacrificed the necessary work of development in order to concentrate their energies on getting the products – tin and wolfram – of which the government stood in grave need for use in munitions making. This fact gives the Cornish miners an undoubted claim to national assistance now, and they are far more deserving of it than the coal miners... are of the ten millions which the Government has given them not to keep the wolf from the door, but merely to ease down the transition from the state of extravagance and luxury in which so many of them indulged during the war to the plainer living with which they will have to put up with now peace is restored. On their merits above there is no comparison between the moral deserts of the Cornish tin miners and the coal miners, and it is a glaring injustice that while the government has voted the latter something like £7 per head, the former should be left entirely to the charity of the public or the humiliating action of the Poor Law.

RECORD CENSUS [These are the figures from the national census undertaken in 1921]:
Total for Britain 42,767,530
FIGURES FOR CORNWALL
Decreases in mining towns.
Cornwall decreases over 7,000 [compared with the figure from the previous census undertaken in 1911]

The figures for Cornwall show a decrease of 7,539. The population is now 320,559, of whom 141,460 are in the municipal boroughs and urban districts and 179,699 in the rural districts. The decrease in the former is 4,934, and the latter 2,605. There are 25,525 more females than males in the county.

The biggest fall is Penzance's 1,382, followed by Camborne's 1,247 (pop: 14,582). Redruth (pop: 9,920) has declined 894, St Just (5,036) 727... Redruth rural shows a drop of 1,211...

The Cornish Post and Mining News – Saturday 18 March 1922:

CASE FOR THE TIN MINES.

SHOULD THE GOVERNMENT STEP IN?
ANCIENT INDUSTRY GOING TO RUIN

(From the "Pall Mall Gazette")

Should the Government step in to save the Cornish tin mines which, since the war, have collapsed, and are in peril of total extinction?

...A case has been fully and lucidly prepared by Mr. Herbert Thomas, a well-known Cornish journalist, who has been pleading the cause of the mines and the miners for a considerable time... Up to the present all efforts to secure financial aid have failed, and Mr. Thomas is pressing for consideration of a far-reaching scheme he has materialised from various views put forward, with the object of saving the mines from destruction.

The Government, it is urged, should in duty bound grant such aid. It is alleged that it is entirely due to Government policy during the war that the present impasse has arisen, inasmuch as, it is argued, the mines were crippled in order to sell cheap controlled tin to America while, at the same time, a high controlled price for coal was demanded to help colliers and coal owners...

Upon this allegation the Government is being called upon to pay a capital sum of £250,000. It is believed that the public would contribute a further sum if the Government set the example, and it is urged that if the Government paid £500,000 it would only be an act of just reparation for the loss sustained during the period of control.

To force home this point, Mr. Herbert Thomas declares that 3,000 unemployed Cornish miners and their families at 30s. per week per family would consume nearly £250,000 in twelve months from Government doles and donations. A grant of this amount from the Government as reparation would restart every Cornish tin mine and employ every tin miner...

Up to now the Government have taken the stand that no fund is available, and that it is creating a precedent.

To this the tin mine advocates point to the aid granted the coal trade, the dye industry, and agriculture.

The Cornish Post and Mining News – Saturday, **28 December 1935:**

MY CHRISTMAS MESSAGE – FROM A CORNISH FIRESIDE TO KINSFOLK EVERYWHERE

SO THIS IS CHRISTMAS!

...We deplore the continuance of War in any part of the world; for the many millions of unemployed, or ill-paid people in almost every country, need the combined and friendly help of the leaders in every part of the world to improve their

condition and stabilise peace and prosperity... as we emerged from the World War in 1918 it seemed possible to unite the great and smaller nations in a League of Nations... the United States quickly realised that the application of the terms of the Covenant [of the League] might easily involve them in a European War, and they side-stepped the Covenant... some big Powers have either defied the League, or left it...

But while these great national and international problems cannot be solved by the man-in-the-street and tax the wit and wisdom of the greatest experts, we realise that we are greatly concerned with the welfare of our own people – at home and across the seas. It is good to know that on November 25th there were 10.5 millions of insured persons employed in Great Britain, and that this was 315,000 more than a year ago. The unemployed (1,918,562) are 292,223 less than a year before. Unfortunately more than 6,000 of these are in Mid-and West Cornwall; and if the advocates of unrestricted competition... succeed in their aim, with the aid of Siam and the Belgian Congo, we may find it difficult to maintain, much less expand, our Cornish tin mining industry; but the international issues are beyond our control.

I do not think I can do better than end these notes with the wise words of the late Lord Courtney of Penwith, a great Cornish Worthy:

"The force which really governs the world is the force of morality. It is this moral force on which we build; it is through moral force we shall win the victory."

Herbert Thomas

The Cornish Post and Mining News – Saturday 1 April 1944:

CORNISH MINES RECONSTRUCTION

– Policy Advocated by County Advisory Committee
Fruits of Two Years Investigation

[The Committee was presided over by the Lord Lieutenant, Lt. Col. E.H.W. Bolitho; its report was submitted to Lord Woolton, Hugh Dalton, President of the Board of Trade, and Sir William Jowitt. The Committee members included A.K. Hamilton Jenkin, author of *The Cornish Miner*; A. Treve Holman, director of the Holman engineering works; W.E. Sevier, Geevor Mines; and G.W. Simms, Tehidy Minerals, Geevor Mines and Malay Properties.]

As a member of the Cornish Chamber of Mines and as a voluminous writer on Cornish mining problems and troubles during the past Half Century, I [Herbert Thomas, the Editor] welcome this report which has the object of preserving... and increasing the prosperity of an industry which has a list of 600 names of Cornish mines – some shallow prospects, others including the deepest tin mines in the world.

The Committee concluded that 'British non-ferrous mining will become extinct – unless the Government intervenes on the termination of the war.' It did not go so far as to recommend the drastic step of nationalization [the socialist solution] but urged a setting up of a Metalliferous Commission, with Regional Committees, to foster the metallurgical industries – funds in block grants should be made available from the Treasury to support mining enterprises.

As far as Cornwall is concerned, the first charge on the capital should be the maintenance as producing concerns of the Geevor (tin), South Crofty (tin and arsenic), East Pool (tin and wolfram) and a wolfram mine.... These mines employ some 1,300 persons, with a gross working expenditure of approximately £500,000, which money circulates in the county for the benefit of the community.

In the years immediately before the war, all these mines were working at a profit – but post-war, costs will be higher – ore-treatment research is needed to improve the amount of tin extracted from the ore (around half at present) – large scale maps should be prepared to enable the more efficient and greater extraction of tin, benefitting employment in the county.

These proposals offer a blend of Private Enterprise and Public Ownership which will be for the good of the country. We presuppose the full cooperation of Labour and so Labour should be represented on the Commission and on the Regional Committees.

As a veteran – almost an octogenarian – free-lancing mining journalist, born in the suspended Gwennap copper and tin mining district, who spent seven years in mining offices, before entering on half-a-century of journalistic work, I should like to endorse these recommendations.

In 1939 an eminent authority on Cornish mining gave it as his considered opinion that if the State had assisted the industry so as to maintain it at its 1919 level until the year 1937, the cost to the taxpayer would have been about £1,700,000 for the 19 years. If we take the number of men employed in it at the beginning of 1919 and the number of men who have gone out year by year up to the end of 1937 and allowing that one-third of the men had obtained other work, the amount that would have been paid out in 'dole' would probably have amounted to approximately £2,323,000 taken at 25s a person per week. This Authority stated that if the above is a fair comparison, the taxpayer was out of pocket over these years to the amount of approximately £600,000. Thus, to assist the tin industry would have been a business proposition, and would actually have saved the ordinary tax-payer substantial sums...

In mid-Victorian days, the Mines of Cornwall directly employed 25,000 to 30,000 persons and had an annual output of £2,000,000 at a time when the purchasing power of the pound sterling was much greater than now. Owing to the exhaustion of the shallower mineral deposits, and to the increased mechanisation of modern mining techniques, we do not expect that the employment capacity of Cornish Mines could again be raised to the Victorian level without subsidies of unduly large proportion, but it could certainly be substantially raised above the present level with profit to the Nation.

We are "moving with the times", and more of my hopes and plans may be realised in the next decade. Meanwhile I can congratulate those presenting a valuable Report to the Government, and only regret that certain strangers to Cornish mining were not aided by a large number of actual Cornish Mining Experts, as it is possible that they would have prevented the closing and dismantling of some of our mines during the stress, strain and losses of men and employment during the present War.

Perhaps at the eleventh hour the tin industry may be saved from becoming moribund and Cornwall from becoming mainly a Pleasure Resort, remembered only as a land of Rest and Beauty.

The catastrophic years of 1921 and 1922 in Cornish tin mining, when mines were shut and miners unemployed, have already been referenced (see above, pp.150-151). The *Cornubian and Redruth Times* source from August 1921 spells out the seriousness of the situation from the Cornish perspective. Local unemployment was 'acute, distressful and deplorable.' What was to be done? In a patriarchal society, when a solution to a problem is needed, there may well be a turning to a father-figure. So it was when the Camborne Mining Division Unemployment Committee, in an act of touching if perhaps misguided faith, decided to send a letter to Mr. Lloyd George, the prime minister, seeking a remedy to the suffering of local men and women and their families. Unfortunately for the Committee members, the prime minister was in no hurry to reply; his continental holiday preparations seem to have taken priority over any interview with those who represented Cornish tin mine interests. Lloyd George was not likely to make an exception for the Cornish tin industry when national funds were so limited in the aftermath of the Great War – and no exception was made when the prime minister's reply by letter came in October that year (see *The Western Morning News*, 11 October 1921, referenced by Kudo, 2015).

Nevertheless, there are ways in which this Committee letter does show how far horizons had widened compared with the parochial world-view evident for much of the Victorian period. Now, in 1921, the urban and rural elites in Camborne, Redruth, and St Just, and their surrounding areas have united in a common cause. There is a mutual recognition of the need for assistance from the Government in London. However, not all within the Cornish elites shared that view. Colonel Francis Freathy Oats, who had taken over the family quarter share of the ownership of the Levant Mine when his father died in 1918 (see above, pp.180), remained a free-market man opposed to any government subsidies as his letter referenced in the Source shows. He castigates such assistance as the 'squandering of public money.' Yet others denied they were looking for subsidies; instead, they were seeking what Herbert Thomas, the Cornish newspaper proprietor, called a 'just reparation.'

Herbert Thomas (1866-1951).[42]

Herbert Thomas's argument focused on the 'moral deserts' of the Cornish tin miners. They were entitled to be treated as an

---

42   The Man in the Panama Hat [Herbert Thomas, Editor of *The Cornishman* newspaper] by Leonard Fuller (1891-1973) Oil on canvas, Penlee House Gallery & Museum, Penzance ©The Artist's Estate

exceptional case, not least because of their 'patriotic efforts to serve this country during the war.' Thomas contrasts the favourable way in which the coal miners were treated both during the war and now in 1921 with the 'glaring injustice' apparent in the Government's treatment of Cornish tin miners. The wages of coal miners during the war were higher than those of tin miners; necessary developments by the owners of the tin mines were put on hold in order to extract as much tin and wolfram as possible for use in munitions manufacturing, leaving the mines ill-equipped to survive the post-war economic downturn. The coal mining industry was now in receipt of £10 million from the National Government, according to Thomas, which worked out at around £7 per coal miner in national assistance.[43] Where was the justice in denying Cornish tin mining national assistance? It meant leaving tin mining families to get whatever came their way either through the 'humiliating' benefits obtained from the operation of the Poor Law or from the charity of those who chose to give from their own wealth.

A year later, with the Cornish tin mines 'in peril of total extinction' according to *The Cornish Post and Mining News* in March 1922, Herbert Thomas used the pages of his newspaper to further develop the case for Government aid. He referenced the Anglo-American deal that helped ensure the American entry into the war, noting that Cornish tin mines were 'crippled' in order to sell tin cheaply to the USA at the same time as coal prices were kept high to help colliers and coal owners. He continued to press the moral case: the Government is 'duty bound' to grant the aid that is needed.

---

43   £10 million in 1921 = c.£625 million today; £7 = c.£438 today

The Government should therefore pay £250,000 to a fund to assist Cornish tin mining in the expectation that an equal amount would be forthcoming from the 'public' (whoever that body might be is not clear). If the Government were to double that sum and pay all the £500,000 that Thomas calculates would bring life back to the tin industry, it would only be 'just reparation' for what was lost due to the Anglo-American deal.

Herbert Thomas went further and showed there was an economic case as well as a moral one. The 3,000 unemployed Cornish miners with their families would consume nearly £250,000 in a year from Government doles and donations, set at the rate of 30 shillings per week per family.[44] If the Government gave a grant equal to this amount to the Cornish tin industry, it would 'restart every Cornish tin mine and employ every tin miner.' Such an argument may foreshadow the Keynesian economics that underpinned the American New Deal in the 1930s – but it carried no traction in Britain in the 1920s.

The writing was already on the wall for the Cornish tin mining industry, in the absence of creative economic thinking at the level of National Government. The 1921 national census figures showed the decrease in the population of Cornish mining towns to be around 7,000 compared with the 1911 decennial census (see the source above). Camborne's population now stood at 14,582, a fall of 1,247 from the 1911 figure; Redruth's population was recorded as 9,920, with Redruth urban showing a decline of 894 and Redruth rural a fall of 1,211 since 1911; St Just's

---

44　£500,000 in 1921 = c.£36 million today; 30s = c.£109 today

population was now 5,036,727 less than in 1911. This was a Cornish region in economic meltdown, facing population decline and crippling unemployment as the staple industry of tin collapsed.

By 1935, the effects of the 1929 Wall Street Crash in the USA had wiped out, across the capitalist world, any economic recovery experienced after 1922. The Cornish tin mining industry had been brought to its knees again – and the indomitable Herbert Thomas is still doing whatever he can to champion its cause. In his 1935 Christmas message to the readers of *The Cornish Post and Mining News*, he laments the plight of the 'many millions of unemployed, or ill-paid people in almost every country' and yearns for an international peace in which world leaders will work together to improve the condition of those in need. He even quotes a so-called 'great Cornish worthy', the late Lord Courtney of Penwith, who had claimed that the force which 'really governs this world is the force of morality.'

Such optimism seems to fly in the face of the grim reality of a traumatic Great War brought about by imperial competition; the economic, social and personal crises caused by the crash of international capitalism in 1929 and the Great Depression that followed; and the consolidation of fascism in Italy, Germany, and Japan in the aftermath of war and economic crisis. Yet Herbert Thomas was far from alone in asserting that the solution lay in a return to a more moral world. In 1938 the influential Moral Re-Armament group was founded in Britain by the American Lutheran Christian, Frank Buchman, and soon became an international movement. His was an evangelical crusade that believed moral recovery was the necessary foundation for a return of economic prosperity. The problems facing the world derived not from the contradictions of capitalism but the failure of people (most of whom, of course, were working class) to live the best lives possible. It was, unsurprisingly, suppressed in all countries subject to Nazi occupation and totalitarian government.

It was not 'moral force' that led to the recovery of national economies. A number of factors were at work, not least what later became known as the 'military-industrial complex'. In fascist and democratic countries alike, across the globe, rearmament brought more employment, as did the expansion of armies. Meanwhile, more than six thousand Cornish unemployed in mid- and west-Cornwall were subject, in the words of Herbert Thomas in this Christmas message in 1935, to 'international issues... beyond our control.' He at least did recognise that the suffering of Cornish families was due to factors other than any failings in moral rectitude.

If the determination of Herbert Thomas to save Cornish tin mining seems 'indomitable' in 1935, by 1944 his efforts appear even more extraordinary as he still battles, aged nearly eighty, to preserve the ancient industry against all the odds. He was convinced there were fresh grounds for hope. *The Cornish Post and Mining News* in April 1944 published the findings of a Cornish County Advisory Committee Report that had been two years in the making and was now advocating, as the end of the war and victory came nearer, the reconstruction of Cornish tin mining. There were powerful Cornish voices and interests at work on this Committee: its chairman was Lt. Col. E.H.W. Bolitho, the Lord Lieutenant of the County of Cornwall; other members included A. Treve

Holman, the director of the Holman engineering works in Camborne, two representatives from the management of the Geevor mine, W.E. Sevier and G.W. Simms, and the local historian, A.K. Hamilton Jenkin, who had written the acclaimed history: *The Cornish Miner* (1927) – see above, pp.59-67.

The Committee's Report and Recommendations were warmly endorsed by Herbert Thomas:

The Committee recognised that Cornish tin mining would 'become extinct' without Government intervention at the end of the war.

The Committee declined to recommend the socialist solution of nationalization and instead proposed 'a blend of Private Enterprise and Public Ownership' through the establishment of a Metalliferous Commission with Regional Committees, all with worker representation.

Such a Commission should be able to draw on funds made available from the national Treasury.

The focus for this new funding should be the four mines which were being worked at a profit immediately before the war: Geevor (tin); South Crofty (tin and arsenic); East Pool (tin and wolfram), and an unnamed wolfram mine.

The Committee emphasised the importance of these four mines for the Cornish economy. They employed around 1,300 persons and had a gross working expenditure of around £500,000, which circulated in the county 'for the good of all.'

Herbert Thomas, in his editorial, provides the figures that highlight the extent of the decline in the Cornish tin industry. In the 1860s, the mines of Cornwall had employed between

25,000 and 30,000 persons and had an annual output of around £2 million – a sharp contrast to the position in 1944 when only three named mines are seen as viable in a post-war world and not many more than a 1000 people out of a Cornish population of around 340,000 are employed in the tin industry.[45] Thomas accepted that Victorian levels of employment and productivity would never again be reached but still hoped for a lifeline from the Government 'with profit to the nation.' But he knew how moribund the tin industry had become. His last line in the editorial carries a prophetic insight with its candid acceptance that Cornwall was on the brink of becoming 'a Pleasure Resort, remembered only as a land of Rest and Beauty.'

The research and conclusions of Norikazu Kudo (see above, pp.150-151) show how the tin industry continually sought Government assistance in the inter-war years – largely without success. The industry continued in its overall decline, subject to the global market price of tin at a time when the high-cost lode mines of Cornwall could no longer effectively compete with low-cost enterprises such as Malayan alluvial mines. Kudo cites the words of Ernest Brown, the Secretary for Mines (1932-1935), in a speech to the mining people in Camborne recorded in *The Cornishman and Cornish Telegraph* (7th March 1935):

> '*The fact was that while the subject of Tin was of tremendous importance in the mining district of Cornwall, the output of Cornwall was but a small fragment of the world total, and the Cornish industry*

---

45 £500,000 in 1944 = c.£28 million today; £2 million in 1860 = c.£322 million today

*was almost entirely dependent on... a certain price
level for the metal in the world market.'*

Such a view had become the received wisdom of the governing
elites in Britain and not without reason. Kudo notes that
Malayan mines had a dominant position in the world
tin market; he also records that British capital had a large
investment in Malaya. Since Malaya was part of the British
Empire, the interests of Cornish tin mining communities
would always be trumped by market forces working within
British imperialism. Kudo draws attention to the fact that
Cornish investors in tin mining also had interest in mines
in Malaya. Over 8,000 tons of tin were produced in Malaya
by Cornish-controlled mines in 1929. Such mines were low-
cost producers who could typically make a profit even when
the price of tin was around £100. By contrast, the Cornish
mines' break-even point was well over £200.

In the severe economic crisis of 1920-1921, when
Cornish mining was on the verge of dying and 3,600 miners
were out of work in the Redruth, Camborne, and St Just
regions, William Bridgeman, the Secretary for Mines (1920-
1922), had spoken in Parliament to reject the call for national
tin controls. He echoed the prevailing economic orthodoxy.
Such a course would be ill-advised since most tin was
produced within the British Empire. Cornish tin production,
as Bridgeman pointed out, was not likely even in the most
favourable circumstances to meet more than a fraction of the
home demand (*Hansard*, 1 July 1920, referenced by Kudo).
Cornish tin output was only one to two per cent of the total
world production.

When the Great War ended in 1918, fewer than twenty

mines remained active in Cornwall, and several of these were in no condition to continue. J.A. Buckley in *The Cornish Mining Industry – A Brief History* (1992/2002), pp.42-44, notes that by 1918:

'The great Basset group of mines had closed... Dolcoath looked to South Roskear (Mine) for its future, sinking a new 2,000 foot shaft there between 1923 and 1926. By the end of the 1920s the company was running out of cash, had found insufficient good grade ore, and failed to get extra backing. The 1930 tin crisis closed the operation finally, as it did most of the (remaining) Cornish tin mines.... East Pool... by the end of the 1930s was all but finished. Only government intervention during the 1939-45 war prevented the mine closing. At the end of hostilities support was withdrawn and East Pool closed.'

With East Pool shutting down in 1945, the only two other named mines central to the 1944 Committee's Report and Recommendations for Cornish Mines Reconstruction still operating were South Crofty and Geevor. By the end of the century, they too had gone. Geevor closed in 1991 and has now become a tourist attraction; South Crofty shut in 1998. Cornish tin mining had finally come to an end.

In this last century of tin mining, at least three generations of Cornish families had experienced the realities of lives shaped by factors largely beyond their control. Their futures were largely in the hands of Government, whose response was shaped by global market prices. Kudo concludes that Cornish mining could not survive without national subsidies.

If the Government chose not to channel public funds into Cornish mining, another option would have been to move redundant miners to other sectors of the economy using public money for training and investment. Governments, however, dithered – and in Kudo's concluding words:

'Cornish miners and their dependents who lived on the dole and sometimes were forced to make decisions whether to emigrate or not were probably the most suffered [sic] people... during the inter-war period. They lived in the world of alternating between hope and despair.'

Sharron P. Schwartz and Roger Parker's comprehensive *Tin Mines and Miners of Lanner – The Heart of Cornish Tin* (1998) – see above, p.149 – provides substantive detail to show the effects of this drawn-out end-time upon a Cornish mining community in a village near Redruth during the inter-war years. In my Overture, I stated that: 'I want to recreate the past in such a way that my tale is faithful to the historical record and, at the same time, enables you to be present in that past' (see above, p.2). To that end, Schwartz and Parker's work provides a vivid insight into a destitution common across the tin mining regions of Cornwall, as these extracts from pages 238-239 illustrate:

'Joseph Cock, the Chairman of the Central Relief Committee [for the Camborne, Redruth and District Relief Fund] made... an impassioned plea to the Cornish worldwide [in the Cornubian, 16/6/1921]... Everywhere there is "a shortness of things"...'

'A central food depot was established in May 1921, and by June had distributed 1,000 parcels, each valued at 5 shillings, to needy families in our district...'

'The Government did eventually help Tresavean [the village mine] financially with a loan of £25,000 in 1922, but even with its reopening... the writing was on the wall. Tresavean closed for good in 1928, throwing numerous Lanner men out of work. In the great global depression of the 30s... much hardship prevailed, and a soup kitchen was opened in the village at the former Miners' Arms public house...'[46]

'One woman in the village, [according to private correspondence received by the authors] whose absent husband was working overseas but sending irregular remittances, was so poor that she was forced by sheer necessity to entertain gentlemen. After such visits, her boys would be seen with a new pair of shoes, or a new jacket, or cap...'

There are stories from those hard times, still half-whispered even in the village today, of known cases of infanticide and burials of babies in the back hedges of cottage gardens. In the light of such hardship during this end-time for Cornish mining, the ethical question I posed in the Overture still remains central to the purpose of this book: 'Should the pursuit of profit ever be at the expense of health, well-being, and life itself?'

---

46   5s in 1921 = c.£15 today; £25,000 in 1922 = c.£1.8 million today

In a society that is structured around the pursuit of profit in privately-owned industries without adequate state regulation, the historical record indicates there are unfortunate consequences for most people in such societies, especially when global market forces work against the speculations of adventurers who risk their own capital but remain uncaring about the fate of others whose labour they need for their enterprises.

FINALE

In my Overture to this work, I promised a tale that would be faithful to the historical record and, at the same time, enable you to be present in that past. I want to bring the past alive, not least so we can learn lessons. I was therefore delighted when Professor Doug Raber in the USA, one of my three readers who comment on each chapter as I write, gave me feedback that indicated I had succeeded in my aims. In October 2022, he commented:

> *'You've got the book going now, especially with the detail of the miner's lives. I'm getting a vibe what it was like to be a miner in Cornwall and I don't think you can do better than that. And it makes your political point without trying.'*

In April 2023, after he had read my penultimate chapter, Professor Raber wrote:

> *'The chapter is evocative. The sense of neglect and what seems to be systemic lack of care is tangible... care [has*

become] a charitable expression, directed at individuals who lose lives, husbands, brothers, and friends in mining disasters. Then they become the "deserving" poor. Outside of that context is an institutionalized and explicit lack of care for mineworkers as a category of human beings. Until one dies, they exist in the minds of the owners and maybe ordinary people merely as objects. Dehumanized until death. And then it doesn't matter.'

It is clear that Doug Raber has made his own judgement call when faced with my ethical question: 'Should the pursuit of profit ever be at the expense of health, well-being, and life itself?' He, like me, is in favour of life and against the unregulated pursuit of profit. I wonder where you stand on these matters, having followed my idiosyncratic path through a couple of centuries of Cornish tin mining history?

I had claimed in the Overture that such concerns could not be more vital since: 'The industrial revolution that began a quarter of millennium ago in Britain now threatens to extinguish our global existence as a species.'

Do you think that claim is valid?

Do you see a link between the existential crisis we are now facing, due to industrialisation and urban development, and the crises endured by those working in the Cornish tin industry in the period covered by this book, *Mine to Die?*

I do.

Let me be transparent. I am a Quaker socialist. I find profound wisdom in the words of the radical Jewish carpenter-turned-preacher, Jesus of Nazareth, who warned two millennia ago that it was even harder for a rich man to enter the kingdom of heaven than it was for a camel to the pass through the eye of the needle – most likely a reference to the very small Needle Gate in the walls surrounding Jerusalem. In other words, that passage was very difficult indeed. Jesus knew what was causing the rot in his pre-industrial world: the pursuit of profit was as destructive then as it is now. Paul of Tarsus, the persecutor of Christians who had become such an influential defender of the subversive ideas of Jesus, caught the essence of Jesus's insight with these words:

'The love of money is the root of all evils.' (1 Timothy 6:10)

It seems to me that recognising the personal and social damage caused by an inadequately regulated pursuit of profit is the vital first step which will enable political actions to mitigate the consequences of such greed.

And so, to the conclusion. It would be a failing if I did not leave the final notes of this Finale with the man to whom this book is dedicated, the former Chief Surveyor and Relief Mine Captain at South Crofty Mine in Camborne: John Toman.

In the early summer of 2022, John – then aged eighty-three – was my guide as we explored the sites of mines at Geevor and Botallack. The pleasure and pride that John feels for his lifetime in mining was crystal-clear, as was the respect he has still for the men he knew in that career, which began in 1960. The miners he remembers were men of charisma and strength, with such talents of brain and brawn. They were, of course, so young too.

John paid handsome tribute to his boss in those early days, the late Jack Trounson, who earned such renown in the mining community and was later a president (1981-87) of the Trevithick Society, which had been formed in 1969 to honour Cornwall's greatest engineer, Richard Trevithick, a key figure in the development of high pressure steam and its application in engines for mining and transport use. John recalled the interview for his first post at South Crofty when Jack Trounson asked his first question.

'Which chapel do you worship in?'

Jack was a man of God, too.

By the time John started his mining career, working conditions had improved dramatically, but there was still the risk of ill health and death. The men whom John remembers could not sustain their feats as drillers, blasters, and stopers beyond their thirties; they finished their time on the surface as general labourers. The strength and health of those men who worked and filled and emptied the trams on the tramways, deep down in the mine, also failed eventually.

John told me this striking story about trammers, numbers of whom were Italian by birth:

"I was waiting for the bus at Penzance quite recently and this older man was next to me in the queue. He turned round and said: 'Where are you from?' and I said, 'St Ives – I'm going back home.' I could tell from his voice that he had Italian blood in him.

"'What about you?' I said. 'Where are you from?' He replied that he lived in Penzance now, in a big house with his family, but he had lived in Camborne.

"I said, 'What did you do? And he said, 'I worked as a trammer at Crofty.' I told him I had worked at Crofty, too. We worked out that he stopped working at Crofty the year before I arrived. I began to ask him for news of trammers I had known in their prime.

"I uttered the name of the first Italian trammer that came to mind. Back came the reply. 'Dead.'

"I offered another name I remembered. 'Dead.'

"And then another. 'Dead.'

"One last shot. 'Dead.'

"There was a brief silence, and then I asked: 'How come you are still alive?'

"'I only worked there for four years, from 1955 to 1959. What about you? You're still alive.'

"I explained that much of my time was spent above ground because of my work as a surveyor. He nodded. We both understood."

ACKNOWLEDGEMENTS

The debt I acknowledged in my last book, *Dying to Know*, to three special people remains considerable. Jessy Raber and her father, Dr. Howard Pue, in the USA, and Ingrid Helmer in the Netherlands, have remained my literary guides. Howard has contributed his considerable scientific and medical knowledge as needed. Ingrid has experienced illness in these last couple of years and yet has still been able to make significant contributions for which I am very grateful. She has an eagle-eye for error. I wish her well and a full recovery. Jessy, who is an artist by profession, has read and critiqued each chapter as I wrote, saving me yet again from my clumsiness on more than one occasion. I am very fortunate to have such impressive literary supports.

These three readers have now been joined in their voluntary task of keeping a critical eye on my writing by Professor Doug Raber, Jessy's husband. Doug's contribution has been invaluable, too. I am very grateful for his advice and encouragement.

I would also like to acknowledge the part played by the team at Troubador, my publishers. I am in awe of the professional skills of my copy editor, Isabel Hill. My thanks to everyone.

Eighteen of the twenty-seven images that appear in these pages are images that need specific referencing in my endeavour not to infringe copyright and they are listed below. I acknowledge here, with thanks, the permissions that I have been granted for the use of these images:

Tehidy Park and House, Illogan, near Camborne – early 19th century (p.7)

Courtesy of The DiCamillo Companion (with special thanks to Curt DiCamillo for his warm support in our correspondence)

Dolcoath Copper Mine, Camborne – 1831 (p.8)

Wikipedia

Tehidy House still smouldering after the fire in 1919 (p.10)

Royal Cornwall Museum, Truro and licence purchased for its use at sales@mediastorehouse.com

View from Dolcoath Mine, looking northwards towards Redruth in c.1890 (p.19) Wikipedia

Stoping at East Pool Mine Mine, Illogan, taken by J.C. Burrows in 1893 (p.28)

Royal Cornwall Museum, Truro and licence purchased for its use at sales@mediastorehouse.com

Using the rock drill – the 'widow-maker' – in the Dolcoath mine, taken by J.C. Burrows in 1904 (p.30)

Royal Cornwall Museum, Truro and licence purchased for its use at sales@mediastorehouse.com

The Library at Tehidy – c1908 (p.35)
    From the collections at Kresen Kernow – B/55

The Hall at Tehidy – c1908 (p.36)
    From the collections at Kresen Kernow – B/55

The memorial to the 1893 disaster and the location of the Cargodna shaft at Wheal Owles (p.86)
    Permission kindly granted by Julian Hodgson, the photographer, through Flickr.

The stulls at 412 level in Dolcoath Mine, taken by J.C. Burrows in 1893 (p.89)
    Royal Cornwall Museum, Truro and licence purchased for its use at sales@mediastorehouse.com

Treadmill at Pentonville Prison – 1895 (p.107)
    Wikipedia

Colonel Walter Raleigh Gilbert – Chief Constable of Cornwall (p.108)
    British Police History (https://britishpolicehistory.uk) – donation made.

Soldiers from the Duke of Cornwall Light Infantry with abandoned tank – 1916 (p.139)
    Bodmin Keep, Cornwall's Army Museum – donation made.

Recruits to the Duke of Cornwall Light infantry – 1915 (p.143)

Bodmin Keep, Cornwall's Army Museum – donation made.

Tresavean Mine, Lanner – c.1910 (p.150)

Royal Cornwall Museum, Truro and fee paid for its use.

The Man Engine at Dolcoath Mine in 1893 (p.165)

Royal Cornwall Museum, Truro and licence purchased for its use at sales@mediastorehouse.com.

Levant Mine, St Just – scene of the disaster in 1919 (p.166)

Still, taken with my camera, from 'The Cornish Post and Mining News' (25.10.19) in the British Newspaper Archive, accessed by subscription.

Herbert Thomas – the subject of Leonard John Fuller's 'The Man in the Panama Hat' (p.198)

Penlee House Gallery and Museum, Penzance – licence fee paid.

Finally, and very importantly, I acknowledge the special debt I owe my wife, Louise, my *sine qua non*.

TWO OTHER WORKS BY ROB DONOVAN

THE ROAD TO CORBYN

"It's a really interesting and unusual book. A Robert Tressell for our times. There are few higher compliments as far as I'm concerned." Linda Camidge

DYING TO KNOW

"*Poetic, beautiful and shimmering with rage. Dying to Know offers a message of hope for those striving to keep the faith in these unjust times.*" *Deb Jones*

My website has the links for more information and purchase:

www.robdonovan-author.co.uk